Abbreviations and acronyms

ACE	Allied Command Europe
ACCHAN	Allied Command Channel
ACLANT	Allied Command Atlantic
AFCENT	Allied Forces Central Europe
AFNORTHWEST	Allied Forces Northwestern Europe
AFSOUTH	Allied Forces Southern Europe
ARRC	ACE Rapid Reaction Corps
C^2	Command and Control
$C^3(I)$	C^2 and Communications (and Intelligence)
$C^4(I)$	C^3 and Computers (and Intelligence)
CCC	Capabilities Coordination Cell
CD	Common Defence
CDP	Common Defence Policy
CFSP	Common Foreign and Security Policy
CHODS	Chiefs of Defence Staff
CINCCHAN	Commander-in-Chief Channel
CINCENT	Commander-in-Chief Allied Forces Central Europe
CINCNORTH	Commander-in-Chief Allied Forces Northern Europe
CINCSOUTH	Commander-in-Chief Allied Forces Southern Europe
CJTF	Combined Joint Task Force
CJPS	Combined Joint Planning Staff
CNAD	Conference of National Armaments Directors
CSCE	Conference on Security and Cooperation in Europe
DM	Defence Ministers (NATO)
DPC	Defence Planning Committee
DSACEUR	Deputy SACEUR

Abbreviations and acronyms

EAPC	Euro-Atlantic Partnership Council
EASTLANT	Eastern Atlantic area
EC	European Community
EDIP	European Defence Improvement Programme
EP	European Parliament
EPC	European Political Cooperation
ESDI	European Security and Defence Identity
EU	European Union
GDP	General Defence Plan
IBERLANT	Iberian Atlantic area
IEPG	Independent European Programme Group
IFOR	Implementation Force
IGC (PU)	Intergovernmental Conference (on Political Union)
IMS	International Military Staff
INF	Intermediate-range Nuclear Forces
JACO	Joint Armaments Cooperation Organization
LTDP	Long-Term Defence Programme
MC	Military Committee
MNC	Major NATO Command(er)
MSC	Major Subordinate Command(er)
NAC	North Atlantic Council
NACC	North Atlantic Cooperation Council
NPG	Nuclear Planning Group
OSCE	Organization for Security and Cooperation in Europe
PfP	Partnership for Peace
PJC	Permanent Joint Council
PSC	Principal Subordinate Command(er)
R&D	Research and Development
SACEUR	Supreme Allied Commander Europe
SACLANT	Supreme Allied Commander Atlantic
SFOR	Stabilization Force
SHAPE	Supreme Headquarters Allied Powers Europe
SIPRI	Stockholm International Peace Research Institute
SRG	Strategy Review Group
TEU	[Maastricht] Treaty on European Union
UKAIR	United Kingdom Air Forces
UNPROFOR	UN Protection Force
WEAA	Western European Armaments Agency
WEAG	Western European Armaments Group
WEAO	Western European Armaments Organization

Partnership in Crisis

CHATHAM HOUSE PAPERS

An International Security Programme Publication
Programme Head: William Hopkinson

The Royal Institute of International Affairs, at Chatham House in London, has provided an impartial forum for discussion and debate on current international issues for over 75 years. Its resident research fellows, specialized information resources, and range of publications, conferences, and meetings span the fields of international politics, economics, and security. The Institute is independent of government.

Chatham House Papers are short monographs on current policy problems which have been commissioned by the RIIA. In preparing the papers, authors are advised by a study group of experts convened by the RIIA, and publication of a paper indicates that the Institute regards it as an authoritative contribution to the public debate. The Institute does not, however, hold opinions of its own; the views expressed in this publication are the responsibility of the author.

CHATHAM HOUSE PAPERS

Partnership in Crisis
The US, Europe and the Fall and Rise of NATO

Paul Cornish

THE ROYAL INSTITUTE
OF INTERNATIONAL
AFFAIRS

Pinter
A Cassell Imprint
Wellington House, 125 Strand, London WC2R 0BB, United Kingdom
PO Box 605, Herndon, VA 20172, USA

First published in 1997

British Library Cataloguing in Publication Data
A CIP catalogue record for this book is available from the British Library

Library of Congress Cataloging in Publication Data
A CIP catalogue record for this book is available from the Library of Congress

ISBN 1-85567-467-X (Paperback)
    1-85567-466-1 (Hardback)

Typeset by Koinonia Limited
Printed and bound in Great Britain by
Biddles Limited, Guildford and King's Lynn

Contents

Acknowledgments

I am grateful to a number of people for their help and advice at various stages of this project. The study group assembled by Chatham House was a vital source of constructive criticism, and I am indebted to all those who attended our meetings or provided written comments. Several people deserve to be singled out for thanks. Fred Frostic, Michael Mazarr, Michael O'Hanlon, Duke Ryan and Greg Treverton were especially helpful during my visits to Washington DC. Ian Clark, Tim Garden, Stuart Peach, John Roper, Trevor Taylor and Philip Towle read and commented upon part or all of the manuscript. During his Chatham House internship in summer 1996, Stefan Elbe unearthed a wealth of useful material, and his insightful analysis vastly improved my understanding of developing national perspectives. Also within Chatham House, the staff of the library could not have been more helpful and willing, and the editorial and production team headed by Margaret May were second to none. This project could not have been undertaken without the generous support of the United States Institute of Peace, to whom special thanks are due. Any errors of fact or judgment remain, of course, entirely my own.

November 1997   P.C.

WESTLANT	Western Atlantic area
WEU	Western European Union
WMD	Weapons of Mass Destruction

Chapter 1

Introduction: the US-European security partnership after the Cold War

'In an alliance the only safe guarantee is an equality of mutual fear.'
— THUCYDIDES, *THE PELOPONNESIAN WAR*

'... some who have just returned from the border say
there are no barbarians any longer.
And now, what's going to happen to us without barbarians?
They were, those people, a kind of solution.'
— C.P. CAVAFY, *WAITING FOR THE BARBARIANS*

In the record of NATO's protracted efforts to adjust to the end of the Cold War, the spring and summer of 1997 will no doubt be remembered as a particularly lively and formative time. The Alliance's mission of outreach to former Warsaw Treaty Organization adversaries and other non-members led to the signature of the NATO–Russia Founding Act and the creation of the Permanent Joint Council (PJC) on 27 May.[1] A few days later, in Sintra, the North Atlantic Cooperation Council was folded into a brand new body, the Euro-Atlantic Partnership Council (EAPC), offering 'an expanded political dimension of partnership'. The practical, military aspects of outreach would remain the responsibility of the Partnership for Peace (PfP) programme, recently enhanced and now described as a discrete element of the EAPC's 'flexible framework'. In early July, under the auspices of the EAPC, the Charter on a Distinctive Partnership between NATO and Ukraine was signed at Madrid. The Madrid Summit, on 8 July, also saw the enlargement debate take a huge step forward as three countries – the Czech Republic, Hungary and Poland – were invited to begin accession negotiations. After signature of a

1

Protocol of Accession by the three candidates in December 1997, full membership of the Alliance will await ratification of the protocols by the current 16 members. At the same time as these developments were taking place amid considerable fanfare, away from the heat of public and media attention NATO also continued its process of internal adaptation: a complex, long-running and often controversial programme to reconfigure the Alliance's command and control structure and its force posture.

A great deal was achieved by mid-1997, but much remains to be done. The PJC, for example, must now demonstrate that a constructive, stable relationship between NATO and Russia is indeed possible. If it is to be credible and useful, the EAPC must show itself to be more than just another long-term waiting-room for NATO membership. Ratifying the admission of three new members could be a contentious and divisive process; the Alliance has more or less promised to complete the formalities by April 1999 – the fiftieth anniversary of the signature of the North Atlantic Treaty – but national debates could generate a variety of obstacles and delays. Furthermore, the enlargement debate is likely to remain lively and controversial for many years to come; the Madrid Summit declaration made clear that enlargement would not be a single event, and that there would indeed be future invitations to join the Alliance. And finally, although it had been hoped that the details of NATO's new command structure and force posture would be agreed early in 1997, the results being announced with a flourish at the Madrid Summit, this was not to be. The internal adaptation programme continued to absorb a great deal of official and political time and attention, nationally and at NATO, and the best hope after Madrid was that outstanding issues could be resolved by a new deadline of December 1997.

Continued discussion of NATO's membership and functions must be expected, therefore. But discussion itself – however vigorous and heated – ought not to be taken as a symptom of an alliance in terminal decline, or at best languishing in the doldrums. NATO has known controversy, often over fundamental issues, throughout its history, inspiring a cottage industry of jeremiahs. On several occasions in the early 1990s, NATO's prospects appeared far from promising, with charges of indecisiveness, lack of leadership, and institutional obsolescence flying around Europe and back and forth across the Atlantic. As disagreement deepened over the Yugoslavia crisis, the transatlantic security partnership looked for a while to be on its last legs. The partnership endured its most serious assault in November 1994 when, as a result of congressional pressure, the

2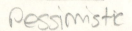

Clinton administration announced that it would no longer help to enforce the UN arms embargo on the Bosnian government. Britain and France protested that in this event their lightly armed troops deployed on UNPROFOR peacekeeping tasks would be made vulnerable to Bosnian Serb attack. This prompted the leader writer of the normally cool and calm *Economist* to ask whether NATO governments would look back on this 'bombshell' as 'their first formal parting of the ways', and 'the beginning of a rift that fatally weakened their alliance'.[2] Some months later, the US announcement was described with even more finality as 'the last straw, breaking the back of allied unity'.[3]

At the same time as its operational credibility was being questioned, NATO also had to face challenges from a number of actual or supposed rival institutions. The CSCE/OSCE has determinedly established a niche for itself in the spectrum of Europe's 'interlocking' security institutions. And the prospect of a European 'identity' or 'expression' in matters of defence and security has become, for many NATO members, much more than the peripheral matter it had been during the Cold War; the EU and the WEU have both secured their places at the negotiating table. NATO has also suffered from the credibility crisis affecting national defence planning. Demands for cost-cutting and expectations of a so-called 'peace dividend' ran high in the early 1990s. Defence ministries and military planners faced the discomfiting prospect of retrenchment somehow becoming constant practice, rather than an occasional necessity. They had reason to be perturbed. In an international environment in which 'threats' would no longer be clear and unambiguous, and in which military planners would have to be content with the somewhat more nebulous notion of 'risks', the scale and quality of armed forces required by a modern state became, conceptually and politically, an open question: 'There is broad consensus that an ill-defined uncertainty and unpredictability are the paramount threats to stability. But how many divisions does uncertainty have, and why are current alliances essential to counter it?'[4] Put another way, 'there is no longer any substantial political support for military planning based on specific threats . . . But there is no obvious way to set spending levels or design a force structure without reference to a specific threat.'[5] The Alliance has also faced a persistent intellectual assault from those who predicted, and have become stubbornly attached to, NATO's demise after the breaching of the Berlin Wall in November 1989 and the dying of the Cold War. The Warsaw Treaty Organization struggled on until its collapse on 1 July 1991, and within six months the Soviet Union had followed suit. Arguably, by the end of 1991, NATO was no longer threatened and had therefore lost its essential Cold War *raison d'être*. Certainly, if NATO had performed like other military alliances in history, it would have faded away soon after the collapse of its main adversary. OPTIMISM .

But in spite of all these challenges NATO has survived, albeit as something of an historical novelty – a military alliance which is organized in time of peace with no foreseeable, unambiguous military threat to any of its current members. The Atlantic Alliance now appears to be in better health than for several years. There are several explanations for NATO's refusal to fade into history. The first, and simplest, is that after decades of cooperation between the United States and its European allies, NATO just had too much institutional inertia for it to be discarded easily and quietly. Another is that the Cold War did not give way, as some hoped and expected, to a new era of stability and predictability in Europe. On 25 June 1991 Slovenia and Croatia announced their intention to leave the Yugoslav Federation, and tension in the Balkans soon ignited into open conflict. August 1991 brought the abortive 'coup' in Russia, giving the impression, which has lingered ever since, of dangerous instability in that country. Thus, while NATO officials were adding the finishing touches to their new, post-Cold War 'Strategic Concept', to be released at the Rome Summit in November 1991, Western governments could hardly have been more aware of the value of formal defence and security cooperation.

A third, more abstract, explanation is founded on the notion that ideas have a part to play in military alliances; NATO did not collapse when the threat disappeared, because kinship – shared ideas, values and experiences – helped to sustain it. The claim has often been made that NATO has been, since its foundation, not only a military alliance but also a community of shared values, historical, political, cultural and economic. Certainly, the preamble to the North Atlantic Treaty of April 1949 expressed the signatories' determination to 'safeguard the freedom, common heritage and civilization of their peoples, founded on the principles of democracy, individual liberty and the rule of law'. And in Article 2 of the treaty the evangelizing signatories committed themselves to 'bringing about a better understanding of the principles upon which [their free] institutions are founded'. After the Cold War, the transatlantic sharing of 'Article 2 values' almost became a value in its own right, to be safeguarded against the dark forces threatening to dismantle the Atlantic Alliance.

If the enlarged, adapted NATO finds itself in need of a new emblem, it could do no better than choose the phoenix rising from its own ashes. Javier Solana, NATO's Secretary-General, could detect the renaissance of the Alliance by late 1995. Reflecting upon the European security debate since the end of the Cold War, Solana wrote of 'a period of highs and lows, of creative thinking and institution-building, and of much rhetorical flourish'. Against this unpromising background, Solana nevertheless saw 1996 as an imminent *annus mirabilis*; 'This time of talk and transition is now coming to an end. Indeed, 1996 could be the year in which practice finally replaces theory and the pieces of a new European security architecture can begin to come together.'[6] Solana may, with hindsight, have expected too much of 1996, but his optimism seems less out of place in the light of events in 1997. Key to the Alliance's vitality during the Cold War was that it could be the subject of political and military controversy, and absorb and even capitalize upon that controversy, without having its basic rationale brought into question. What appears to have happened by mid-1997 is that, after several years of uncertainty, the Alliance has reconstructed something like its Cold War *modus operandi*. NATO's place at the centre of European security is now more assured than at any time since 1989, and it now has sufficient strength and purpose to enable it to cope with controversy.

Optimism is one thing, complacency entirely another. To secure its place in Solana's 'new European security architecture', NATO has had to find satisfactory, durable answers to two questions: could the Alliance continue to be a provider of security (however broadly defined) in a dramatically altered Europe? and could the US–European security partnership be sustained? The quest for positive answers to both questions has dominated NATO's efforts at outreach, enlargement and internal adaptation. This paper focuses upon internal adaptation; a programme too often eclipsed in the media and the literature by the high drama of outreach and enlargement. But after recent achievements in these two areas it is now especially pertinent to ask what, precisely, the new members will be joining in 1999. What are the results and the deficiencies of the internal adaptation process, and has the process made the Alliance better, or less, able to meet the new challenges of Euro-Atlantic security? The tone of this paper is broadly upbeat, but also cautious; in important respects NATO is actually far from robust and will require careful management for some time to come. Internal adaptation has certainly helped to validate NATO in the European security debate and as the bridge between the United States and its European allies. But the strengths and weaknesses of NATO's internal adaptation can too easily be overlooked or misunderstood. The internal adaptation programme has achieved a great deal but must be brought to completion; however many applicants there may be for membership of the Alliance, it is difficult to imagine an unreconstructed NATO having much of a future.

This book is largely about the inner workings of the Alliance, rather than its external shape and size, and this prompts a health warning regarding the narrowness of analysis confined to institutions and organizations. Institutions, their role and survival, have dominated discussion of European security in recent years; hence the popularity of architectural metaphors. Yet critics have rightly pointed out that preoccupation with security institutions could be an unhealthy obsession with traditional, linear forms of international politics – an 'all-too diverting entertainment',[7] pursued at the expense of addressing more fundamental concerns, and unable to take proper account of the development of new security issues and the forces of economic and political globalization. Volker Rühe, Germany's defence minister, warned how obsessive interest in organizational detail could lead to the important issues of the day being obscured or misunderstood: 'Thinking of NATO's reform only in military and organizational terms means neglecting the fundamentally new political and strategic challenges of today.'[8] Yet institutions do matter, not least for the much-needed practical and intellectual anchor-points they provide during times of turbulence and change. Institutions can also – if managed imaginatively and with flexibility – become a framework which encourages further change, rather than recoiling from it. And institutions provide for diversion and pause; given current uncertainties and the possibly disastrous consequences of misjudgment, tinkering with this or that institution – NATO, the WEU, the EU, the OSCE – might appear a relatively benign occupation, perhaps even one to be encouraged.

NATO's internal adaptation is assessed in the following five chapters. Chapter 2 begins with brief summaries of theoretical reflections on the questions how, why or whether a military alliance should persist beyond the conclusion of its main task, and then suggests that the practical response to these questions has been growing interest in the intriguing idea of a 'virtual' or 'capability-based' military alliance. Theoretical approaches to the study of international affairs are often thought to have little to offer to the 'real' world of policy-making. In this case, however, the theoretical and practical debates overlap to a remarkable – and useful

– extent. And to theorize is, after all, only human. Chapter 3 describes 'four paths to compromise' (the US, British, French and German), without which the goals and complex formulae devised in 1996 and 1997 could not have been agreed. A detailed analysis of the internal adaptation of NATO, up to spring 1997, is offered in chapter 4. Chapter 5 tests the strength of the consensus, in the light of defence, security and defence-industrial thinking and practice on both sides of the Atlantic. Chapter 6 concludes the study.

Chapter 2

Military alliances in theory

Introduction

Military alliances are of interest not only to practitioners in the art – military strategists and defence policy-makers – but also to scholars of international relations. Most students of international relations would be aware of various attempts to impose a theoretical framework on the conduct, character and dynamics of the international system. Military alliances, defence and security feature prominently in these theoretical deliberations. Theory offers many different perspectives on the rationale for, and creation of, military alliances. However, beyond the widely held assumption that an alliance whose original *raison d'être* has ceased to apply is, by definition, surplus to requirements, theory has rather less to say about what should happen once the original rationale fades or changes, or when the alliance has succeeded in its original aim or is becoming obsolete. In this respect at least, theorists and practitioners both find themselves in uncertain waters; but shared uncertainty hardly amounts to the useful overlap between theory and policy mentioned in chapter 1. Happily, this is not all there is: theory may not offer much, but what it does provide can help to explain some of the difficulties in, and to inform the process of, turning a traditional military alliance into something more than a contingent, ad hoc and reactive form of security cooperation.

International relations theory encompasses a vast range of ideas and schools of thought. It is not the object of this chapter to record and evaluate every possible theoretical perspective on alliance termination and adaptation; such a project would unbalance this brief paper and would, in any case, be beyond the competence of this author. Rather, this chapter looks, briefly and selectively, at the problem of the 'threatless alliance' from three perspectives. Military alliances and the use of military force are most readily associated with the sovereign nation-state. *Realism* is the school of thought which places the sovereign state and its security at the centre of an inherently volatile and insecure international system, and is a rich source of opinions on the use of military alliances. Another set of ideas, which may be grouped under the heading *pluralism and liberalism,* goes beyond the confines of the nation-state, challenges many of the assumptions upon which realism is based and offers broader views of the dynamics of the international system and the role of military alliances. Finally, there are those ideas – organized here under the heading *internalism* – which address the inner dynamics and inertia of complex organizations such as NATO. These three perspectives, together with two recent and controversial assessments of the shape and future of the international system, are explored below. As far as NATO is concerned, all point in the same direction; if the Alliance has a future, it will be as an internally rationalized 'alliance of choice' rather than as an externally rationalized 'alliance of necessity'. The final part of the chapter turns to current practice and shows how growing enthusiasm for the 'virtual alliance' is not too far removed from the best that theory has to offer.

Realism

Realism concerns itself with what it takes to be the essential characteristics of states, individually and in their dealings with each other, in an international political system, the principal component of which is the state. For the realist, the state is essentially preoccupied with its interests and territory, and the security of both against actual or perceived threats and challenges. The state is a sovereign body, imbued with a territorial identity and the expectation of non-interference from other sovereign states with which it is on equal terms, legally and morally. The international system in which states survive and function is anarchic rather than hierarchic; there is no political authority above or beyond the state, no world government. State interests are frequently seen as clashing, and individual states are expected to maximize their power and influence in pursuit of their interests. This much could be described as *classical* realism, where states may also seek to optimize, project or protect their national values and interests by cooperating with other states. This cooperation can be expressed in a very broad range of affiliations, alliances and alignments covering all those areas – from telecommunications to trade to tourism – in which states need, or want, to do business with one another. Such cooperation can find expression in loose and occasional relationships, informal and temporary groupings, or formal, treaty-based commitments. Whatever the form of alignment, and whatever the motivation for it, the object of cooperation between states is to maximize state interests to a degree, or in a manner, which the individual state acting alone could not achieve.

The military alliance could be said, therefore, to be a fundamentally realist phenomenon. Sovereign states stress the value of military force – the legitimate use of which is an exclusive prerogative of the state – in guaranteeing the security of their interests and territory. By the same token, military alliances are an important element in the search for, and exercise of, power. Any state unable either to guarantee its own security through its own armed forces or to achieve sufficient power relative to other members of the international system, must seek assistance. And if two or more states face a common threat, the simple need for military assistance can result in a military alliance. The organizations which result are usually found at the more formal end of the spectrum of cooperation between states. Failure to honour a commitment to assist an ally could severely endanger the security of the threatened partner, and military alliances therefore tend to be formal and legalistic. Effective military cooperation can also, however, be achieved in ententes and coalitions which do not conform to this formal, treaty-based model, and history offers numerous examples of secret alliances.

When the commonly perceived external threat disappears, it might reasonably be supposed that, without its basic rationale, the classical realist military alliance would also dissolve. The dissolution of an unthreatened alliance is not, however, an inevitable outcome in classical realism. The argument risks becoming circular, but since the impetus behind the alliance was the convergence of the *interests* of the parties to it (defined in terms of either security or power), as well as the existence of a common *threat*, it is at least possible logically that an unthreatened alliance could be sustained if the parties decided that it remained somehow in their interest to do so.[1]

A military alliance in the classical realist mould need be no more than an ad hoc response to an external threat; it could also be a complex and long-lived structure such as NATO. And it could be used in other ways too if the threat were defeated or disappeared. But in so far as the nation-state is an intellectual construct as well as a geographical, political and legal one, the classical realist's mission to describe states and explain their behaviour towards one another soon becomes a more complex task. In the 350-year-old 'Westphalia system' of international politics, it is not only that territory and trade routes must be protected against marauders, it is also that the *ideas* of state sovereignty and non-intervention must themselves be nurtured. Aggression by one state or group of states against another is not only dangerous for the unfortunate victim, it can also be dysfunctional and fundamentally unsettling to the international system itself. A military alliance can therefore be more than merely a defensive response to aggression; it can also represent the affirmation of the core principles of state sovereignty and non-intervention.

When realism goes beyond the bounds of national policy-making and *raison d'état* and begins to seek more comprehensive explanations for the dynamics of international politics, so a variant of realist theorizing known as *structural* realism comes to the fore. Structural realism is concerned to turn the key realist observations into a coherent theory of international relations, a theory which is positive rather than normative (based on the world as we see it, rather than as we would wish it to be) and with which, if predictions cannot be made, explanatory models certainly can. As in classical realism, the state, preoccupied with security and power, is the leading player in the anarchic international system. But for the structural realist, the state is constrained by the system within which it operates, a system which is characterized by a reciprocating, balancing cycle. The search for security and power, and the military alliances which may result, are more than mere descriptions of ad hoc, unilateral state behaviour. The international system is one in which accumulations of power are *automatically* counterbalanced by groups of states seeking constantly to identify and neutralize imbalances in the system; the military alliance is no mere accident, it is the engine of the international system.

In realist theory, whether classical or structural, there need be no intrinsic limit to the duration of a military alliance: as a classical realist policy preference it may be sustained for as long as is thought necessary, or even put to other uses; for the structural realists, the longevity of an alliance as a defensive, reactive posture is determined extraneously, by the duration of the perceived imbalance in the international system in response to which it was formed. A military alliance could therefore last months, years or even decades, and there is nothing extraordinary in the fact that the transatlantic security partnership lasted for more than 40 years before it began fundamentally to reassess its role in the light of the collapse of the Soviet Union and the Warsaw Treaty Organization. It is at this point, however – when the threat diminishes, and when Thucydides' 'fear' is no longer felt in equal measure by all members – that structural realism becomes somewhat more pessimistic regarding military alliances than its classical counterpart: 'much of the NATO-is-dying analysis stemmed directly from structural-realist theory.'[2] For the structural realist, the function of the military alliance is not simply to provide an ad hoc response to an actual or projected military threat, but to counterbalance an agglomeration of power in the international system. By this argument, the significance of the end of the Cold War was not simply that the military threat had disappeared, but that the bipolar balance had come to an end, and with it the rationale for the transatlantic security partnership. Faced with the uncomfortable prospect of NATO's *survival* after the end of bipolarity – against theory and all the odds – some structural realists respond stubbornly that, logically, the collapse of the Alliance is inevitable, however long it may take.[3]

Another argument within the realist canon is that states do not ally against *power* alone, but against *threats*. In *The Origins of Alliances*, Walt preferred the expression 'balance of threat' to 'balance of power', and noted that the depiction of a state as an actual or potential aggressor involved an examination of that state's military *intentions* as well as its *capabilities*.[4] Most military/political threat and risk assessments would take a similar approach. But Walt then argued that a security alliance formed in response to a threat could take one of two forms: 'When confronted by a significant external threat, states may either balance or bandwagon. *Balancing* is defined as allying with others against the prevailing threat; *bandwagoning* refers to alignment with the source of the danger.'[5] It is not immediately apparent which – if either – of Walt's models is more appropriate for a world with no clear military threats, at least on the Cold War scale. Balancing, which amounts to joining the weaker side against the potential aggressor or hegemon, is hardly appropriate when neither disproportionate military capability nor hostile intentions can be discerned, and may even prove to be inflammatory. This is not to say, of course, that there will never be calls to counterbalance states which are powerful and unmatched, but not militarily aggressive or expansionist; there currently exists a widespread perception of the United States as an 'unbalanced power in the world'.[6] Bandwagoning, on the other hand, suggests attraction to malign strength. But, once again, it is difficult to identify a state or force which is strong, certain, aggressive and threatening enough to have such an effect. Bandwagoning – for all its adverse connotations of pre-1939 appeasement – might take place if it were perceived to be a safer, less confrontational option than balancing. But even then, a conciliatory approach to neighbours which are powerful and restless, yet relatively unthreatening militarily, may be difficult to sustain domestically and regionally, as the development of Germany's relations with Russia has suggested.[7]

Realism, with all its emphasis on states, security and threats, might reasonably be thought to provide the safest intellectual refuge for a military alliance facing awkward questions about its future. However, classical realism proves to be no more than lukewarm, and structural realism icy cold, as regards the future of NATO. The best that might be said is that if unthreatened states choose, for their own reasons, to ally or to maintain an alliance, there is nothing in theory which says they cannot. Furthermore, there is nothing in realist theory which says that cooperation could not be speculative, or consist of a series of ad hoc responses to otherwise unconnected crises, although theory offers little advice on collecting these disjointed responses into a reasonably coherent, established framework. It would be incautious to suppose that the future will not contain its share of aggressors and neo-imperialists. Indeed, many commentators argue that one consequence of the ending of the Cold War is that an unusually large number of such characters will appear on the international scene. And it is conceivable that states could decide to balance (or bandwagon) in the face of such dangers, *as they develop*. But if so, the result is unlikely to be the scale and type of military alliance which developed during the Cold War. It may be, though, that the difficulty lies not with realism *per se*, but with the level of analysis to which it has become coupled. If Huntington's forecast of a 'clash of civilizations' has credibility, then something like a realist rationale for military alliances could still be valid.

Huntington's assessment of the course of global politics and the causes of global conflict makes concern about the durability of the Westphalia system appear something of a decadent distraction. 'The fundamental source of conflict', he argued, 'will not be primarily ideological or primarily economic. The great divisions among humankind and the dominating source of conflict will be cultural.'[8] Like Arnold Toynbee in his Reith Lectures for the BBC some 40 years earlier,[9] Huntington warned against Western complacency. The non-Western world, he perceived, was no longer willing to be 'the objects of history as the targets of Western colonialism' and was keen to join the West as 'movers and shapers of history'.[10] Huntington's call to arms to defend Western values could offer some hope for those anxious to find a new type of rationale for a military alliance: military alliances could be driven neither by contingent, state-level power-political interests and assessments of military threat, nor merely by some vague sense of culture and kinship, but by the shared perception of being part of an endangered 'civilization'.

Huntington's thesis seemed to find a ready audience in NATO, and among Western military audiences more generally, which were not slow to examine whether a new style of confrontation might succeed the Cold War. In November 1991 NATO launched its new 'strategic concept' at its Rome Summit. In the document, the term 'threat' made way for the somewhat less precise 'security challenges and risks'.[11] But the document seemed somewhat over-confident when it insisted that 'the new environment does not change the purpose of the security functions of the Alliance, but rather underlines their enduring validity.' Before long, the notion that 'risks' and general instability were enough of a rationale for the preservation of NATO was failing to convince even NATO itself. Early in 1995 Willy Claes, then NATO's Secretary-General, suggested that 'Muslim fundamentalism is now as big a threat to the alliance as communism once was.'[12] Claes' comment was quickly withdrawn and the search for a more convincing (and less inflammatory) rationale went on. Nevertheless, Huntington's thesis has remained a respected point of reference in Western military circles, although his ideas have attracted the attention of a growing chorus of critics.

Among the many responses to Huntington's argument, two main criticisms were that he exaggerated the clarity and validity of 'civilization' as an organizing concept in international politics and that he underestimated the continuing, central importance of the state in the international system.[13] Huntington replied by insisting that 'what ultimately counts for people is not political ideology or economic interest. Faith and family, blood and belief, are what people identify with and what they will fight and die for.'[14] He then went on to assert: 'And that is why the clash of civilizations is replacing the Cold War as the central phenomenon of global politics ...' Huntington may have underrated the significance of 'economic interest' as a factor for armed conflict; it is clear both that economic crises have often contributed directly to the outbreak of conflict, and that harsh economic circumstances can give rise to non-military security challenges. And if access to scarce resources (e.g. water) could be termed an 'economic interest' then the 'civilizations' thesis, far from being alarmist, may in time prove to have been rather complacent. But there are still nagging difficulties with the idea of replacing state with civilization as the level of analysis, and extracting a new, 'macro-realist' rationale for military alliances, with 'Western civilization' confronting 'Islamic', 'Confucian' and other opponents. It is, after all, possible for local loyalties (e.g. family ties), personal convictions (e.g. religious faith) and cultural *mores* to be held without their necessarily resulting in a conflict between, as an illustration, Christians and Muslims. It is one thing for individual and national political behaviour to be, in a general sense, civilizational, but rather another for actions to be guided by direct reference or appeal to civilization itself, and for the result necessarily to be confrontation.

Huntington has asserted, quite reasonably, that cultural self-confidence and anti-Westernism are spreading through much of the non-Western world. What will happen next is much less certain. Most recently, Huntington has argued, to NATO's certain relief, that 'in a multipolar, multicivilizational world, the West's responsibility is to secure its own interests', and that 'in the post-Cold War world, NATO is the security organization of Western civilization and ... its primary purpose is to defend and preserve that civilization.'[15] But, in spite of these exhortations, the 'civilizations' thesis is still too generalized – and perhaps also too 'politically incorrect' – to have a direct and discrete influence on individuals and governments in the West, and to persuade them to man the ramparts. History shows, after all, that beleaguered and declining civilizations are often the last to acknowledge their predicament. For the present, therefore, the 'clash of civilizations' seems unlikely to provide a sufficient rationale for a new, post-Cold War style of confrontation-based military alliance.

Pluralism and liberalism

The second set of views – pluralism and liberalism – offers more diffuse perspectives on NATO's persistence after the Cold War. In these approaches the international system is more than simply the sum of the activities of the individual states which are members of it. Non-state organizations play a part and have a life of their own. The same might even be said of inter-state organizations, which can exist and function without constant reference to, and expressions of consent from, their member states. The state-centric 'Westphalia model', by this view, has rarely if ever been an exhaustive explanation of the international system and faces yet more threats to its credibility. Economic interdependence, transport, the media, telecommunications and the constantly developing

15

international legal system increasingly challenge the image of the international system as an archipelago of self-sufficient, sovereign islands. Alliances and alignments in the international system may (and should) be driven, not just by states, but by all those acting within and communicating across the system: businesses, human rights and humanitarian organizations, and even individual people. It is only by acknowledging the variety and complexity of the international system that it can be reformed and improved. A world view which takes no account of actors and forces other than sovereign, independent states will be unable to break free of the cycle of war and destruction for which states are responsible. Finally, states themselves are more than simply the security-preoccupied governments by which they have usually been represented in the international system; the realist taboo against blurring the boundaries between domestic and international politics must also be broken. States are composed of national, ethnic, cultural and historical groups which interact within the state and with other groups elsewhere in the world. When states form alignments and alliances – even military alliances – it follows that the relationship will be driven, not solely by considerations of power and security, but also by 'softer' cultural preferences and values.

Since the end of the Cold War much has been heard of challenges to the coherence of the Westphalia model, from within and without. The internal coherence of the Westphalia model is scarcely a new issue, however; the model, and the principles upon which it is based, particularly sovereignty and non-intervention, have never been entirely flawless and immune to questioning. The very term 'Westphalia system' is, somewhat misleadingly, evocative of a golden age of harmonious inter-state relations. In reality, though, there have always been violations of sovereignty, violations which the system tolerated for the sake of peace and stability.[16] Furthermore, the environment in which sovereign states exist and operate is changing dramatically, a transformation for which 'globalization' in economy, culture and telecommunications is partly responsible:

> The system of sovereign states … is being undermined both from above and from below. It is threatened from above by two 'revolutions' that affect sovereignty. There is the empirical revolution of interdependence and globalisation that both deprives states of much of their 'operational', that is, effective, sovereignty and transfers many of their previous functions to a largely private world capitalist economy that is beyond national control and under very meagre inter-state control. The other is the normative revolution that erodes

the content of sovereignty and restricts the rights, derived from sovereignty, that states were free to exercise at home – that is the human rights part of the revolution ... The attack from below results from the multitude of totally or partially failed, troubled and murderous states whose claims to sovereignty are either unsustainable or unacceptable.[17]

A related problem is that the post-Cold War 'international' system is witness to many tensions, crises, conflicts and cases of aggression taking place *within* states, rather than between them. One popular view is that the Cold War produced a global hegemonic framework which imposed stability upon tense regions or, in certain circumstances, allowed instability to develop into conflict, thereby permitting the controlled release of pressure from the central confrontation. With the end of the Cold War, the framework has gone, the cork has been removed from the bottle, and numerous latent 'ethnic' conflicts have sprung up all around the world, with no framework to impose moderation or control.

According to the most recent annual survey of the Stockholm International Peace Research Institute (SIPRI), however, this view is somewhat alarmist. In 1996 there were 27 'major armed conflicts' in progress around the world, a reduction from the 1995 figure of 30;[18] in 1989, which SIPRI describes as the 'last year of the Cold War', the number of conflicts was 36. These figures suggest a steady downward trend. Furthermore, of the 27 conflicts listed for that year, SIPRI could trace the origins of 22 back to before the end of the Cold War in 1989: 'This remarkable continuity means that conflicts initiated after 1989 have to a large degree been contained.'[19] The SIPRI survey therefore does not support the view that the international system is sinking into complete disorder and violence. There was some bad news, however. The SIPRI survey is far from complacent, warning that the nature of conflict is of greater interest than its scale. All but one of the major armed conflicts in 1996 were intra-state, rather than inter-state – the exception being the recrudescence of the conflict between India and Pakistan over Kashmir. Suggesting that 1996 might have seen 'the end of the post-cold war period', SIPRI described a new style of conflict involving issues 'more local in nature, such as religious, ethnic or other identities', 'social and political instability', 'a lack of state legitimacy' and 'state failure'.[20] States or organizations wishing to intervene in such conflicts, perhaps in order to restore law and order, would require a new approach to conflict and its resolution. In their 1996 survey, SIPRI described 'major power involvement' in post-Cold War conflicts as 'shifting from active support of one fighting faction against another to attempting to contain and minimize violence in localized conflicts'.[21] In other words, states would have to respond to these conflicts for reasons and in ways which did not fit easily into the realist mould, not least because the 'threat' is remote, as is the 'balance' which has been upset. It is difficult to see how a military alliance created to meet circumstances such as these could be formed from the traditional, threat-based mould. But a military alliance which was, somehow, flexible in its structure, and saw its function as combating instability rather than a specific enemy, might be more apposite.

The lesson of the pluralist outlook, therefore, is that the international system is continuing to evolve and move away from Westphalian state-centredness. Since it is within the Westphalian model that the rationale and modalities of military alliances have traditionally been identified, advocates of NATO's continued utility after the Cold War might do well to be more versatile and adventurous in their thinking. But, as with the various forms of realism, pluralism does not exclude the notion of an unthreatened military alliance.

Liberalism's response to the claim that the 'traditional mould' for military alliances is deficient would be to argue that the fault is with the contents as much as with the vessel, and to stress the need to acknowledge the cultural values, affinities and preferences which operate within, between and across states. International alignments and alliances are formed and sustained for many reasons other than the security and defence of the sovereign state, its territory and interests. Even military alliances have a positive, progressive dimension; more than a community based on a common threat, a military alliance can (and must) be a community based upon shared historical, cultural and ideological experiences and values. But the notion that 'soft' ideological and cultural considerations can *contribute to* the coherence, stability and endurance of a military alliance (rather than, *pace* Huntington, serve as the *main rationale* for a military alliance) is hardly new. Since the earliest days of the Cold War the Western doctrine of containment was both geopolitical and ideological, in that the Soviet Union was seen both as an imperialist, expansionist power on the fringes of Europe, and as a totalitarian/ communist challenge to Western civilization. Throughout the Cold War, NATO exemplified the closeness of this relationship between military threat and ideological confrontation. What enabled NATO to be sustained for so long – particularly during periods of détente when declarations of imminent military danger lost some of their force – was, in part, the underpinning of kinship and ideological solidarity.

Liberalism has evidently had an important role in reinforcing a military alliance, but whether it can provide a sufficient rationale for a military alliance is another matter. It is one thing to assert that the Western/liberal-democratic/free-market ideology emerged intact, dynamic and self-sufficient from the Cold War – 'The "West", i.e., the group of developed democracies, as such does not need an enemy, in communism, Islam or anything else'[22] – but it is more difficult to see what this robust Western ideology can do for military alliances when it finds itself with no 'alliance of necessity' to underpin, and no worthy ideological opponent. The history of the Cold War shows that, for all its intellectual self-sufficiency, when faced with the more practical task of shoring up NATO Western liberalism became dependent upon an intellectual, political, economic and ethical opponent. Ideology helps to explain the long-standing antagonism between the leaders of the two Cold War alliances: 'The difference between the United States and the Soviet Union has been less in their behaviors than in their ideologies. Each sought to make other countries over in its own image.'[23]

Just as the prospect of an unthreatened military alliance creates difficulties, so it is hard to conceive of Western liberalism underpinning a military 'alliance of choice' when it sees no ideological and moral adversaries on the horizon. Without at least some sense of distinctness, if not of danger, it may be difficult to find a convincing ideological rationale for 'a defence alliance that everyone wants to join'.[24] The question is, therefore, whether Western liberalism can provide a sufficient, objective and (in contrast to Huntington's concept) *passive* rationale for a 'hard' military alliance such as NATO. Although normally soft and shapeless, viscoelastic substances such as egg custard and silicone putty become formed, firm and resilient when subjected to sudden stress. Can NATO behave like egg custard? If not, must it be admitted that 'An "ideal" NATO is probably beyond the reach of member governments today'?[25] Liberalism could, perhaps, make a more positive contribution to the cohesion of NATO either by emphasizing pre-existing differences between members and non-members or by manufacturing some altogether new sense of cultural or ideological distinctness. But the outcome would seem to differ little materially from the realist perspective. If the difference is one of scale, there is a risk that, where military alliances are concerned, liberalism becomes merely an anaemic reminder of Huntington's 'clash of civilizations'.

The proposition that liberalism has not merely emerged intact from the Cold War, but is now in the ascendant, with the world happily and/or inevitably homogenizing along Western liberal-democratic lines, offers intriguing challenges for those seeking to establish a constructive relationship between liberalism and NATO as an unthreatened alliance. The end of the Cold War has been acclaimed in triumphalist terms for one reason or another: as a validation of the concept of nuclear deterrence; as a demonstration that NATO had 'worked' since it had 'kept the peace in Europe for forty years';[26] as a victory for spiritually based societies and cultures over those of a secular orientation; as a victory for capitalism over the command economy; as a victory for individual rights and liberties over statism and repression; and as a victory for nations over empires. And then there was the biggest triumph of all – the 'triumph of liberal democracy'.[27] But if liberal democracy 'won' the Cold War, and if liberal democracy is an innately pacific ideology,[28] what could be the rationale for the post-Cold War continuance of a military alliance such as NATO?

The debate over the 'triumph' of liberal democracy was fuelled by a celebrated article written in 1989 by Francis Fukuyama.[29] In this article Fukuyama touched upon the question of democracies' propensity to go to war, and in a subsequent amplification of his controversial argument noted that 'the virtues and ambitions called forth by war are unlikely to find expression in liberal democracies.'[30] But, contrary to the accusations of complacency with which many critics responded to his 'thoroughly improbable' thesis,[31] Fukuyama did not suggest that this was either a preferable situation or one which could endure. In the first place, although democracies would not fight each other, they could find themselves in conflict with non-democracies (though presumably only until these societies had accepted their liberal-democratic destiny). He had, too, some sympathy for the idea that the absence of military threat and mortal combat could make people, communities and states weak, dispirited and incoherent and, in the end, prone to collapse. In the complete absence of any threat, the creation and management of military alliances would not be thought necessary. But if suddenly it did become necessary to forge a military alliance, perhaps because the very meekness of the state invited opportunist aggression by a dishonourable neighbour, the moral deficiencies and material inadequacies of the state would make alliance worthless or impossible. As to the prospects for harmonious, liberal-democratic international life, Fukuyama was again far from complacent, arguing that the liberal-democratic triumph might create its own challenge, that people might become bored and 'struggle for the sake of struggle', *against* 'peace and prosperity, and against democracy'.[32] Fukuyama warned that 'dissatisfaction arises precisely where democracy has triumphed most completely: it is dissatisfaction *with* liberty and equality. Thus those who remain dissatisfied will always have the potential to restart history.'[33]

If the conditions which undermine the rationale for, and substance of, military security and military alliance-seeking also bring in their train a new sort of threat, then 'triumph' is perhaps the least appropriate term to describe Western life after the Cold War. Yet, in spite of Fukuyama's admirable wish to hedge his bets and keep alive at least the *idea* of bodies such as NATO, the 'end of history' looks ominously like the 'end of military alliances'. In an ever more homogeneous world, even if pacific, liberal-democratic governments could be persuaded to keep their powder dry, they would do so in anticipation of a wholly unknown type of 'threat' or 'enemy' of which they can have had no experience; it is not easy to see what kind of values and interests will be defended - by whom, with whom and against whom - when the danger to be confronted is that of a 'nihilistic war against liberal democracy on the part of those brought up in its bosom'.[34] And therefore it is not easy to see how a military alliance such as NATO could be based either upon the innate and triumphant qualities of liberal democracy or upon its internal tensions. The Alliance could, at best, be seen as a means to maintain the Western security community, the members of which have renounced the use of force in their dealings with one another and are opposed to the 'nationalization' of defence policy and military capability. NATO's value as an 'inclusive or inward-oriented security regime' should not be underestimated, particularly as it extends its collective security function through the PfP programme, the EAPC and the enlargement process.[35] But it is difficult to envisage an organization of the character, complexity and financial cost of NATO being rationalized exclusively along these lines; and if this *is* to be NATO's destiny, it will face stiff competition from the OSCE.

Internalism

The third set of views to consider are those which seek to explain what is taking place, and what the future might hold, from the perspective of the Alliance itself. Decision-making theory challenges the notion that decisions (in, for example, foreign and security policy) are made by monolithic, hierarchical governments acting entirely rationally and predictably. It stresses that government is divided vertically into

21

departments, each of which may approach a problem or crisis in a different way. The outcome of this process – the decision or policy – is likely to be some form of compromise between these different elements and their respective approaches. And since government departments react to change by using existing 'standard or routine operating procedures', there is a tendency in this 'organizational process' model of decision-making for the outcome to be cautious and incremental, 'except when a major disaster occurs'.[36] Decision-making theory also introduces the human element into the equation, by showing that governments and their subordinate organizations are composed of individuals and sets of individuals who have their own interests and prejudices.[37] In this 'bureaucratic politics' model, where government is dissected horizontally, decisions are shaped through bargaining between one set of interests and another.[38] Once again, the outcome or decision is likely to involve an element of compromise between many different interest groups.

Just as the 'rational actor' thesis can be challenged, so too can the 'rationality' of a military alliance, in two ways. Decision-making analysis is of value generally, in understanding how NATO functions, in all its complexity. It also helps us to understand, more closely, how NATO has so far avoided the fate which might, 'rationally', be expected of an unthreatened military alliance. The organizational process model suggests that NATO would adapt cautiously and conservatively to the end of the Cold War. Over time, NATO's risk-averse internal adaptation, in which it has gradually accreted new roles while being reluctant to drop old ones, appears to have borne fruit. But it was precisely this conservatism which prompted frustration and gloom in some analysts: 'While telling them-selves and their shareholders that they [organizations] are briskly responding to new challenges, they adopt incremental change that in the end is too little, too late. Such is NATO's present path.'[39] The inference to be drawn from this is that the end of the Cold War has not, in organizational process terms, been a 'major disaster' for NATO. The lesson of the bureaucratic politics style of analysis is that NATO is a complex bureaucracy, composed of individuals and interest groups who must be expected to have an interest in their incomes and careers and therefore in the 'survival' of the organization in which they are employed.

Taken together, these schools of decision-making analysis suggest that NATO has avoided oblivion through the strength of its organizational 'survival instinct'. To talk of the 'survival instinct' of an inanimate construction might be to plumb the shallows of anthropomorphism. Nevertheless, the idea is useful, and may provide a clue as to NATO's immediate prospects. It can be argued that the 'survival instinct' expresses itself in three consecutive phases: resistance to, and scepticism towards change; affirmation of the use, value and potential of the organization (particularly as regards the financial costs of establishing a new or rival organization); and finally, acceptance of change and adaptation to it. The final phase – adaptation – has an air of opportunism about it; the organization will adapt either by expanding its function (taking on new tasks) or by increasing its membership and base of support.[40]

NATO could be said to have become an inter-state organization with a 'life' (or at least an inertia) of its own. The consent and active participation of member states are obviously crucial to the origin and function of such an organization; but at some point the organization may become less than entirely dependent upon the goodwill and support of its members. This is not to suggest that NATO could function without the agreement or support of its members, but rather that the Alliance has become a 'player' in the process, in its own right and with its own voice. Over time, organizations can develop their own interests and priorities which may or – crucially – may not coincide with the interests and priorities of member states.

The theory of international institutions takes issue with this organizational approach.[41] No organization can be sealed hermetically from the preferences, decisions and actions of its members; a more interactive model is therefore required. Institutional theory accepts that the organization will adapt and modify, and may even be assigned to previously unimagined tasks. But because the organization is part of an 'open system', in which its members have a key role, it is more readily seen as an instrument than as an actor in its own right; the main determinant is not the *survival* of the venture, but its *utility*. By this view, NATO could be used by its members to forge links with other bodies – state and non-state – or even for 'domestic' purposes, as a means to control the behaviour of allies.[42] The new jobs for the old alliance need not be security or defence-related; in terms of NATO's founding treaty, new tasks taken on in pursuit of the idealism and 'soft security' of the Preamble and Articles 2 and 4 could be just as admissible as those aimed at furthering the 'hard' security of Articles 3 and 5.

In the search for a new rationale for NATO, or for military alliances in general, theory is, plainly, not much of a substitute for threat. Realism has little of a positive nature to say about the survival of an unthreatened military alliance, although the idea of a military alliance at least remains crisp and intact. Classical realism suggests lamely that an alliance may survive, provided member governments find some use for it. Structural realism finds it unlikely that the post-bipolar alliance could withstand the inevitable reordering of the global power balance, but is reluctant to give a date for NATO's inevitable demise. Looking beyond the confines of the power and interests of the state, and the threats it faces, it might be thought that the Alliance's liberal-democratic ideological underpinning could be expanded into a rationale in its own right. But there are difficulties with this proposition; and it might, in any case, involve venturing too far into the realms of 'soft' security which could be an insufficient basis for the day-to-day running of a taut and efficient military alliance. Analysis of NATO's inner dynamics presents a cautious, conservative and opportunist organization, but does at least allow for the Alliance's tasks to be redefined and for it to be given new momentum.

None of the theoretical models discussed entail the immediate end of the Alliance, but neither do any of them offer a compelling and sufficient rationale for the Alliance's survival after the Cold War. It is at least clear what post-Cold War NATO could *not* be. With no ideological and military confrontation, NATO could not continue as a traditional military alliance. And NATO could hardly be considered an alliance if its collective action were to be entirely ad hoc, contingent and reactive. There may, nevertheless, be enough middle ground on which to assemble a makeshift rationale. There is, at present, no call for NATO as an externally rationalized 'alliance of necessity'. But as an internally rationalized 'alliance of choice', NATO could still have the substance it needs to survive. The culture and ideology shared by most of NATO's current and proposed members could act, passively, to complement the practical side of the organization, the need for which will remain. NATO's members can confidently expect further calls for the use of military force in situations far short of all-out, collective defence under Article 5. Furthermore, given declining defence budgets and the reluctance of national politicians to pitchfork their countries alone into an international crisis, NATO members will be unable and unwilling to act other than collectively even in these lesser crises. NATO's members already have common cause, and anticipate the need for cooperative action. The final element of the improvised rationale requires the collective adversary to be defined in general – even abstract – terms, rather than as a specific military threat. Thus, the Alliance's 'enemy' might become 'instability' (or weapons proliferation, the narcotics trade, piracy and so on) into which NATO members might be drawn or against which they might wish to intervene.

In the 'alliance of choice', NATO members have a satisfactory, theoretical response to the question 'why should NATO survive?'. The Alliance's rationale thus could be jury-rigged, although most or all of the crew would have to demonstrate their eagerness to keep their ship afloat by bailing constantly. The question 'how should NATO survive?' elicits a comparable response in practical, politico-military policy-making circles. A cooperative, do-it-yourself mentality is energizing NATO, transforming it into a 'virtual alliance' for 19 or more members, some with long-standing loyalties and bonds, and others new to the team. 'Virtual NATO' is consistent with the makeshift rationale described above, and shares many of its vulnerabilities.

Virtual alliances

The basic function of a military alliance is to provide security and stability for its members. Alliances have, usually, been built in response to an external threat: when the threat disappears, alliance members are in a stable and secure position and have no need for the alliance which might therefore be dissolved. If, however, members still wish to retain some form of security cooperation – either to meet lesser dangers or to provide an insurance policy against major threats in the future – an important question soon emerges. To what extent is it possible to have cooperative military security available on call without the constant underpinning of an external threat? Is it possible for the broad, fluid and often contentious debate about security threats, challenges and risks to be somehow detached from the more concrete matters of military preparation and readiness? In the present context, budgetary pressures alone render most Western states unable to achieve their military security objectives other than by cooperating with like-minded states. But without the unity of purpose imposed by an external threat, can a way be found to enable such states to cooperate? There are two possible ways of achieving such cooperation. The first is to make the alliance less territorial in its orientation (an approach favoured by several US analysts, as Chapter 5 will show), possibly by adopting various technological advances. The second, making virtue out of necessity, is, rather than waiting for an overwhelming and unifying threat to materialize (or, worse, inventing one), to build the alliance around the abilities and strengths of its members to carry out certain (undefined) operations.

A non-territorial alliance

Territory – and how to protect it – is key to understanding the development of military alliances during the Cold War. An important contribution made during the Cold War to the history of military alliances was the practice of stationing troops on the territory of allied states in peacetime (or something like it). With the exception of the Dutch Barrier in the eighteenth century, this was an unprecedented method of meeting alliance commitments.[43] The number of troops permanently based overseas has fallen dramatically in recent years. US bases in the Philippines have been closed, and those in Germany, the UK and elsewhere have all been reduced. Budgetary constraints seem likely to push the 'draw-down' process still further, as might environmental protests such as those seen in Germany, and anti-American protests of the sort witnessed in Okinawa. Britain, Belgium, Canada and the Netherlands have also withdrawn some or all of their forces from Germany, and Russia has removed its groups of armies from central Europe.

The decline of foreign basing has prompted a search for alternatives. One possible course is to make use of largely unpopulated islands and territories, such as Diego Garcia and Ascension Island, or even to build huge floating air-bases off-shore, such as that being considered for Okinawa. However, the alternatives to foreign basing, particularly those proposed by the United States, are increasingly technological. The speed, range and accuracy of modern weaponry suggest to some that the best response to sporadic aggression in the future would be to launch a handful of cruise missiles: a 'surgical strike' in which no US or allied aircrew would be needlessly endangered. As well as developments in cruise missile range and targeting, consideration is being given to the production of 'arsenal ships' – enormous, 800 ft surface ships with as many as 500 missile launchers, capable of supporting operations at sea and on land, and providing surface-to-air defence. The US Department of Defense's 'Joint Vision 2010' is clear as to the military and economic advantages of a technology-based strategy: 'The combination of these technology trends will provide an order-of-magnitude improvement in lethality. We will be able to accomplish the effects of mass – the required concentration of combat power at the decisive time and place – with less need to mass forces physically than in the past.'[44] Defence ministries around the world are becoming steadily more focused upon 'power projection' as the new rationale for weapons and equipment procurement, with strategy designed around the idea of 'disengaged' conflict, 'a war fought from a distance that proceeds without a massing of troops and weapons. Missiles fired from hundreds or thousands of miles away, or even from the continental US, might converge on a single location or several strategic targets at once. In this long-term scenario, aircraft carriers, tanks, fighters and bombers may cease to have a primary role in the postmodern theater of war. Most US forces might be stationed at home'.[45]

Territorial aggression is still the main (albeit not the sole) concern for defence ministries and military strategists, and will be for the foreseeable future. The 'postmodern' strategy, however, is effectively *non*-territorial. In this regard, there are striking similarities between the expectations currently held of arsenal ships and modern missiles on the one hand, and on the other the priority accorded to strategic atomic air power in British and US military planning in the early years of the Cold War.[46] Now, as then, a yawning credibility gap soon emerges. The credibility and reliability of US interest in, and commitment to, west European security during the Cold War was in large part the result of the permanent, peacetime stationing of US ground and air forces along the Central Front; without such a presence, the fear was that the Alliance would become 'decoupled' as soon as any fighting began, if not before. But if, in the age of super-accurate, long-range missiles, military intervention with or on behalf of an ally were to be no more than the projection of military power by air or sea, perhaps with the telegenic insertion of limited ground forces for the duration of the crisis, then military alliances might still be possible, but only as a less binding, pre-Cold War type of 'paper agreement'.

A highly technological strategy might be the best – or even the only – response to aggression and crises in the future, but military alliances built around such a strategy will almost certainly prove to be less robust, convincing and durable than the Cold War version. Even in the unlikely event that the United States and its European allies were to become cooperatively and contentedly 'postmodern' in their strategic thinking, the credibility of the Alliance could be undermined in a different way: through dependency. Given their individual budgetary positions, west European governments are most in need of security and defence cooperation. But, other than in relatively peripheral areas such as humanitarian assistance where they may wish – and be able – to organize on their own initiative, high-grade power projection would have to be 'borrowed' from the United States. The 'postmodern' strategy sits at the peak of an extraordinarily sophisticated and costly US R&D pyramid. European R&D is far behind and could approach the US effort only if national budgets were pooled. Yet the same west European governments so in need of security and defence cooperation (among themselves, and with the United States) have so far been unable or unwilling to contemplate the creation of a European defence R&D base.

As chapter 5 will show, this ambivalence finds few sympathizers in the United States, where sensitivity to suggestions of free-riding by America's European allies runs high. If allied contributions to a high-technology, non-territorial strategy are so unequal, then Clausewitz's famous dictum, regarding the inseparability of military matters and political discourse, might be brought into question. This might cause some anguish for Western military elites steeped in Prussian wisdom; 'Military structures should conform to political structures, for military action must be in pursuit of a political aim and must be subject to political direction.'[47] For, instead of conformity between the political and the military, a rift could form. Through their technological dependence on the US 'postmodern' strategy, the European allies could come to see NATO as the source of security *capability*, while they (the European allies) continued to debate and pursue a security *policy*, albeit without any real substance. This would mean that, in time, NATO's efforts to become 'more political'[48] after the Cold War (and thereby conform to changing political structures) would have been undermined as a large section of the transatlantic political structure – NATO's European members – conducted a private debate. In such circumstances, NATO would become little more than a military warehouse, decoupled in the Clausewitzian sense, and it is inconceivable that such an arrangement could be accepted in the United States as the basis for a security partnership.

A capability-based alliance

As the large-scale military threat to Europe diminished, so it became clear to defence ministries that a different rationale would be required for national defence planning and equipment procurement, if cost-cutting finance ministries were to be kept at bay. One solution was to make defence planning less a relatively simple matter of structuring forces as a response to explicit external threats than one of assessing the range of likely or possible military commitments (described in general, neutral terms), and creating a suite of military capabilities which could meet most or all of those commitments. The switch from 'threat-based' to 'capability-based' military planning was championed by the British

Ministry of Defence in its 1993 Defence White Paper.[49] The result was a complex framework (gradually simplified since) involving 'defence roles', 'military tasks' and 'multiple earmarking', in which balance and flexibility would be key. But, as well as being over-elaborate, the framework also threatened to distort the relationship between political guidance and military planning:

> As we continue to refine the audit of our Military Tasks, we are faced with the need to make investment decisions which will pre-figure our force structures. The result of this process is the admission of 'capability based forces' into the defence vocabulary. While this is an admirable attempt to reconcile force structures to Military Tasks, which in turn should derive from political ends, the develop-ment of these forces is a hedge against the diversity of those political ends. Thus as a result of the more opaque strategic conditions which we now face, we are seeking to create forces which are ubiquitous and capable of discharging tasks across all Defence Roles. The danger in this is that our focus shifts from political ends and towards military means and so corrupts the relationship between the two elements of strategy.[50]

There are also concerns that the capability-based approach, which (in spite of the dangers cited above) could function well enough at the national level, might be inadequate at the level of multilateral security cooperation. The object of versatile, capability- rather than threat-based, multilateral security planning would be to organize an appropriate military response to a crisis as it developed. Yet, however spontaneous the crisis, the military response itself could not be entirely ad hoc; some joint and combined training, liaison and operational planning, and extensive coordination of intelligence and communications would be necessary before any amount of interoperability could be achieved. It could even be argued that ad hoc interoperability requires more, rather than less, preparation than routine military cooperation. It might, of course, be possible for two or more states to organize a genuinely spontaneous military response at short notice, but the practical complexities of military cooperation suggest that operations of this sort would be either ineffectual, or low-key affairs. For the exercise of multilateral security policy to be politically, militarily and financially effective and efficient, there must be some military coordination and preparation. Rather than taking place in a political vacuum, preparing to be militarily interoperable, or even anticipating a need for military cooperation, is itself a political act. It is difficult to conceive of an effective, combined military resource existing without a level of consensus having been reached politically. If political direction is confused or uncertain, or if the debate is institutionally separated from the military capability, the combined effort will flounder.

Conclusion

Theoretically and practically, it is difficult to find a foolproof rationale with which to sustain defence and security cooperation between the United States and its European allies. Yet it is possible to cobble together something passably effective; the 'why?' and the 'how?' of NATO's survival can both be answered reasonably well. Theory and practice could both, to some degree, be satisfied by an 'alliance of choice' which had for its rationale the institutionalization of planning for ad hoc operations and which based its strategy on the capabilities of its members rather than on the threats and dangers they expect to meet. But, if taken to the extreme, an alliance based entirely on its military capabilities could see the vital politico-military relationship being eroded. Non-territorial, technological solutions could be useful, but they also threaten to undermine the idea of a transatlantic security partnership. Furthermore, this fragile, composite rationale will require the positive support of members of the Alliance. Whatever the limitations and flaws, many things are possible if allies choose to cooperate. Without a return to Cold War-like circumstances, nothing more should be expected; the case for a transatlantic military alliance will not be self-evident but must be deliberately assembled.

Chapter 3

Four paths to compromise

*Pressures on NATO.
bullet point*

Introduction

The end of the Cold War was an awkward moment for NATO, as uncertainty over the need for complex and costly military security alliances deepened. Serious disagreements between the allies over their involvement in former Yugoslavia exacerbated the situation. NATO also faced a fundamental, institutional challenge, in the form of mounting pressure – particularly from France – for a 'Europeanist' (rather than 'Atlanticist') approach to European security after the Cold War. France had withdrawn from the Alliance's integrated military structure in 1966, had ever since questioned US dominance in European security structures and had been deeply suspicious of the idea that the sovereign French government's duties of national defence could properly be subsumed into a collective effort. After the Cold War, it was not long before France began to speak of European defence cooperation outside NATO 'in more far-reaching terms than ever before'.[1] The US response to the latest heresy was curt. In March 1991 – in an act curiously evocative of US Secretary of State Dulles' December 1953 warning of an 'agonizing reappraisal' of the United States' commitment to European security if European allies did not begin to work together – US Under Secretary of State Reginald Bartholomew sent a 'Note' to European capitals. In this document Bartholomew made it plain that while the United States would welcome a European voice in NATO, it was still uneasy about the prospect of a European security caucus within the Alliance, possibly based on the WEU, which could browbeat the United States.

The conflict between the 'Atlanticists' and the 'Europeanists' over the basic character of Europe's security – and who should pay for it – had been a perennial feature of NATO politics during the Cold War. But for some observers, the end of the Cold War was a watershed in institutional terms, and for them the uncertainty and mounting intra-Alliance disagreement of the early 1990s could only point towards Europeanization of security thinking and practice. Traditionally the champion of Europeanism, France saw the end of the Cold War as an opportunity to shift the locus of European security planning and organization back to Europe. Britain, carrying the Atlanticist standard, argued that the basic character of NATO and the US involvement in Europe should be nurtured in uncertain times. At the time, the only point of agreement between the two sides was that defence cooperation should not be a matter for supranational policies but should remain inter-governmental. The result was the compromise offered in the December 1991 Maastricht Treaty. The treaty created the inter-governmental Common Foreign and Security Policy (CFSP) and spoke of the 'eventual framing of a common defence policy, which might in time lead to a common defence'. The WEU was brought back into the picture to become, in an imprecise and politically flexible formula, 'the defence component of the European Union and ... a means to strengthen the European pillar of the Atlantic Alliance'.

The developing Atlanticist/Europeanist tension was best illustrated by the rush to provide Europe with a new, multinational intervention force. In May 1991 NATO's Defence Planning Committee (DPC) envisaged NATO's Allied Command Europe (ACE) fielding a large army corps to deal with conflicts and crises in and around Europe. The ACE Rapid Reaction Corps (ARRC), located firmly within NATO's hierarchy and commanded by a British general, duly came into being on 2 October 1992. The ARRC produced an agitated response from France and Germany who saw it not merely as a conspiracy to give the British the best jobs but also, more seriously, as pre-empting any moves towards the creation of a genuinely European force. The result was the Franco-German 'Eurocorps' founded in October 1991, formally established two years later and made operational by late 1995. After heated discussion about whether the Eurocorps would mean divided loyalties and even undermine NATO, in May 1992 Malcolm Rifkind, the British defence minister, accepted that the Eurocorps might, after all, be suitable for WEU operations and need not be considered untouchable by NATO. The following month in the 'Petersberg Declaration', the WEU Council of Ministers drew up a list of WEU missions, taking pains to point out that these would be 'fully compatible' with the primary commitment to

NATO's collective defence structure. The Eurocorps controversy was largely calmed in January 1993 when French and German chiefs of staff struck an agreement with SACEUR over the relationship between NATO and the Eurocorps.[2]

Even in the midst of deep disagreement over the function of the Eurocorps and the issues which lay behind it, it was clearly not impossible to find some workable arrangement. NATO seems to have been extraordinarily adept at institutional self-preservation of this sort. Just as the transatlantic security partnership has been no stranger to disagreements and controversies, so it has also been versatile enough for a way to be found out of the various dilemmas with which it has been confronted. The compromise set out after June 1996 provides additional confirmation of the Alliance's adaptability, and could prove to have been its most accomplished act of self-preservation yet.

At the June 1996 ministerial meeting of the North Atlantic Council (NAC) in Berlin, the idea was finally accepted of establishing the European Security and Defence Identity (ESDI) *within* NATO, and the further development of the Combined Joint Task Force (CJTF) concept was authorized.[3] After the Berlin ministerial, the *Economist* could write more happily of 'genuine good cheer in Berlin',[4] and Hervé de Charette, France's foreign minister, was seemingly delighted that 'For the first time in the history of the Atlantic alliance, Europe can express its defence identity.'[5] The Berlin communiqué – examined more closely in chapter 4 – has the air of a turning-point in the development of European security ideas and institutions after the Cold War. It generated a considerable amount of political and military planning work in the months before the December 1996 meeting of the NAC. Outstanding disagreements – numerous and, in some cases, fundamental – would, it was hoped, be resolved before the next NATO summit meeting in Madrid in July 1997.

If the June 1996 meeting does indeed emerge as a turning-point, it will be seen to have been the culmination of shifting perceptions regarding post-Cold War European and transatlantic security among the four protagonists in the debate, the so-called 'Quad' of key NATO members: the United States, France, Britain and Germany. The remainder of this chapter will summarize each of these positions. The United States grew steadily more reconciled to the idea of closer cooperation among its west European allies in matters of defence and security, even to the extent of developing appropriate European institutions. The British government, traditionally wary of European initiatives in these areas, developed a new, more positive perception of the role of the WEU. France's so-called *rapprochement* with NATO can only be described as a revolution in the politics of Western defence and security. Judging by the amount of heat, noise and exhaust they generated, the United States, Britain and France could fairly be described as the engine of the June 1996 agreement. But there was a fourth protagonist – Germany – whose contribution to the whole process was in some ways the most important. Germany acted as the engine's lubricant; hidden from view, reliable to the point of being unexciting, best kept tightly contained, and crucial to the success of the whole.

The United States and European security and defence cooperation

US views of European defence and security cooperation have been changeable and often confusing, and have been neatly described as 'fiercely ambivalent'.[6] During the Cold War, proposals for some discrete form of European cooperation were not usually met with much enthusiasm in Washington. In the orthodox US view of the security partnership with western Europe, NATO was very firmly at the centre of the relationship and was key both to continental defence and security and to Western coherence in the face of the Soviet threat. Uncontrolled development of European cooperation could, in the US view, undermine NATO's function both as the source of European security and as the linchpin of the Western Alliance. But at the same time, the perennial defence budget debate in Washington pushed the Americans into a more accommodating position. From the mid-1980s, a struggle for resources has taken place between Congress and the administration, with Congress usually gaining the upper hand and allocating a defence budget significantly below that requested by the administration.[7] In these circumstances the US–European burden-sharing debate became a live issue; a greater contribution by European allies was seen as a means to ease some of the military and financial burden placed on the United States for continental European security and stability. The form of European cooperation was in some respects a secondary issue, provided it took place within, and complemented, the broader NATO framework. In blunt terms, Washington was concerned to persuade European allies to *do* more, and was less concerned about the ambition of some European allies to *be* more in an institutional sense.

The beginnings of compromise between Europeanism and Atlanticism could be traced to the WEU Platform on European Security Interests agreed in The Hague in 1987. The US response to the Platform demonstrated Washington's conditional acceptance of European defence and security cooperation. Concerned at the Reagan administration's 'unilateral' arms control successes at the Reykjavik Summit and with the INF Treaty, on 27 October 1987 the nine WEU member states came together to add impetus to the regeneration of the WEU which had begun in 1984, and to ensure that west European perspectives were not overlooked during US–Soviet negotiations.

The Hague Platform stated boldly that 'We are convinced that the construction of an integrated Europe will remain incomplete as long as it does not include security and defence,' and set the goal of a 'more cohesive European defence identity'. [8] But the Platform also acknowledged the commitment to the North Atlantic Treaty, insisting that 'the security of the Western European countries can only be assured in close association with our North American allies. The security of the Alliance [i.e. NATO] is indivisible. The partnership between the two sides of the Atlantic rests on the twin foundations of shared values and interests. Just as the commitment of the North American democracies is vital to Europe's security, a free, independent and increasingly more united Western Europe is vital to the security of North America.'[9]

This form of words, together with the fact that the French government, as a member of the WEU, had joined the Hague Platform, suggested a constructive and responsible approach to US–European security relations and had the effect of 'turning American opinion around in favour of the emerging European Security and Defence Identity'.[10]

From Washington's point of view, an acceptable agenda for European defence and security cooperation was taking shape in the years before the end of the Cold War. It would therefore be inaccurate to see the US as implacably opposed to such cooperation, with some fundamental conversion being required before the Clinton administration could indulge in a 'warm embrace of European unity goals and institutions'[11] and allow the June 1996 Berlin compromise to take place; the US 'path to compromise' was more a matter of confirming existing trends than changing direction. There was, however, a hardening – albeit temporary – of US attitudes towards European cooperation during the Bush administration.

The Bush administration's approach to European security cooperation was influenced by the President's assessment of the crucial contribution to the downfall of the Soviet Union and the end of the Cold War made by the United States, NATO and Bush himself, and by Bush's assessment of the scale of the 'victory' over the West's Cold War adversaries. Sensing a 'virtually unconditional victory in the Cold War',[12] Bush, with the US administration in his wake, became markedly more suspicious of 'Europeanism', seeing a threat to NATO's new role as the stabilizer of the new Europe. NATO, in Bush's view, 'should be at the heart of the new European system' and should enlarge quickly by admitting Poland, Hungary and the Czech Republic.[13] NATO should also resist, vigorously, any attempt to restructure it or to supplement it with new institutions. When, in the uncertain months before German unification on 3 October 1990, Kohl and Mitterrand appeared amenable to Gorbachev's proposals for a unified Germany to be neutral and outside NATO, and even to a 'revamping of the entire European security apparatus once the Cold War was over', Bush insisted that a unified Germany should follow the NATO path rather than 'defect' from the Alliance.[14] Other challenges to NATO's primacy were usually met with a brusque US response.

Yet even while the Bush administration was insisting on an exclusive role for NATO in the security and stability of the new Europe, there was still an undercurrent of opinion that European cooperation could indeed be compatible with US interests and the maintenance of NATO. Severe budgetary pressure led the Bush administration into drawing up the short-lived 'Base Force' concept for controlled budget and force reductions. In 1992 Congress set a ceiling of 100,000 US troops in Europe – some 33 per cent less than the figure requested by Bush. Moreover, Congress began to consider the possibility of a complete withdrawal of US troops from Europe unless European allies absorbed more of the cost.[15] The Bush administration could hardly have been more aware that the maintenance of NATO and the US–European burden-sharing debate were firmly linked. There was also some acceptance that an uncompromising approach to NATO expansion might be inflammatory – particularly to Russia. A more subtle course was that embodied in the NACC: a joint proposal by Bush and Kohl, outlined at NATO's Rome Summit in November 1991 and inaugurated the following month.[16]

The US 'path to compromise' therefore reflected two imperatives. First, congressional insistence on cost-cutting and value for money in defence spending translated into the demand for the European allies to assume more of the financial and military burden of their own defence and security; second, NATO was to be maintained. The European response to the burden-sharing imperative was to contemplate closer cooperation (and, for some, integration) in matters of defence and security in one European forum or another (either the WEU or the European Community/Union). The European response to the NATO imperative was continually to reassure the Americans that more

European cooperation would not undermine, but would actually strengthen NATO. However, when Europeans have collaborated in order more fairly to share the transatlantic security burden between the United States and its European allies en bloc, their efforts have too easily been construed as undermining or rivalling NATO. What was needed, in the US view, was a means by which rivalry could be understood as a managed, constructive and contained response by the Europeans. One solution lay in the idea that if European cooperation could be diverted into peripheral areas of activity, then both the burden-sharing and the NATO imperatives could be satisfied. The idea was summed up by General Colin Powell, Chairman of the US Joint Chiefs of Staff, in a lecture in London in April 1992: 'This new Alliance role in no way prohibits or seeks to discourage a strictly European Security and Defence Identity. On the contrary, it encourages such a development, so long as it is accomplished in harmony with the Alliance. A European security structure would be well suited politically and militarily to handle inter-regional [*sic*] crises, humanitarian actions and peace-keeping tasks'.[17]

Within this framework, Washington's approach to European cooperation in defence and security actually formed a trinity: burden-sharing, the preservation of NATO, and a division of labour at the lower end of the spectrum of defence and security activities. Although it was not long before NATO began to challenge the wisdom of a division of labour between it and the WEU, US thinking on the issue had now matured and the US 'path to compromise' was, for the present at least, more or less complete.

The United Kingdom and the Western European Union

Since 1945, Britain's view of west European defence and security cooperation, particularly when institutional pretensions have been detected, has been variously indifferent and sceptical, cautiously tolerant and openly hostile. The explanation is simple enough. Almost as an article of faith, every postwar British government has stressed the need to sustain US interest in – and conventional military commitment to – west European defence and security. This paramount objective became the unassailable orthodoxy in Whitehall and informed British thinking about, and responses to, proposals to 'Europeanize' the defence and security of western Europe.[18] Britain's advocacy of the Atlantic relationship and the primacy of NATO also brought certain benefits; its influence and interests were nurtured by a privileged position within the Alliance, one which was 'disproportionate to [Britain's] actual political and economic power'.[19]

As a founder member, Britain has always been legally committed to the WEU, and bound by its treaty. But Britain's faith in the forum has been somewhat tepid. Whitehall has characteristically seen the WEU as a means to some other end, rather than as an end in its own right. It is useful to reflect that the WEU only came about because the Churchill government saw an urgent need to prevent Washington's threatened 'agonizing reappraisal' of the US commitment to western Europe in 1954–5, in the aftermath of the European Defence Community fiasco. The last-minute proposal made by Foreign Secretary Anthony Eden was to reanimate the defunct Western Union Defence Organization – the antecedent to NATO, based on the 1948 Brussels Treaty – rename it WEU, and modify its founding treaty. The WEU would then provide the sought-after institutional framework in which to capture and exploit the military potential of a rearmed West Germany, and would demonstrate to the Americans that their European allies were, after all, capable of cooperating in vital matters of defence and security. Once born, however, the WEU had to endure 30 years or so of benign neglect from its parent. And even when, after the reactivation of the WEU in the Rome Declaration of 27 October 1984, Britain became more engaged in the WEU, there was no real change in Whitehall's basic approach: the forum continued to be viewed, constructively or otherwise, as a means to some other end. Since the early 1990s Britain's view of the WEU has certainly become more complex, and Britain has become more engaged in the workings of the WEU – but only because the forum is now seen as a means to reach several goals simultaneously.

The idea of 'managed rivalry', used in the context of US thinking about west European defence and security cooperation, has something to contribute to an understanding of Britain's attitude to the WEU since the end of the Cold War. Britain now sees in the forum the opportunity to shape the debate over the west European security 'architecture' by emphasizing, or imposing upon it, certain political, institutional and military characteristics. Politically, the WEU serves as a model for European defence and security cooperation which is, above all, inter-governmental rather than anything more integrationist or even 'federalist'. It is always difficult, particularly in Britain, to bring more light than heat to discussion of European institutions and the progress of the European project, but in this case the British approach has as much reason as rhetoric in it. The operational deployment of military force, involving the likely death and injury of servicemen and women, must be one of the defining privileges and responsibilities of a modern liberal-democratic government. The established British view is that, in the exercise of that privilege, governments have a duty of care to their forces and must be expected to demonstrate their execution of that duty to the electorate, via Parliament and the electoral process. There is, therefore, a case for ensuring that the privilege is not granted to any body which, through its own inadequacies or its constitutional immaturity, is not able fully and credibly to execute the duty of care. Institutionally, the British government also came to see the WEU as a means to ensure that European defence and security cooperation did not drift too far – geographically and conceptually – from the Atlantic. The WEU was to become, if not the European institution for which the French in particular had called, then a bridge between NATO (still the paramount forum for Western defence and security) and whatever arrangement the west Europeans were able to muster. With this in mind, the British approach had, and still has, no room for the merger of the WEU with the European Union, the particular preference of the Germans. Finally, militarily the British could conceive of a WEU which would have some operational utility without rivalling NATO. In this model, the WEU would be focused upon lower-scale military tasks, would not create its own bureaucracy and command structure to rival NATO, and would rely on forces 'double-hatted' from NATO rather than assigned separately by member governments.[20]

With all these intimations of ulterior motives regarding the role of the WEU, the British 'path' to the June 1996 compromise has to be followed with some caution. Beginning in May 1992, with the British suggestion of a way out of the Eurocorps deadlock, the following brief and selective chronology charts the evolution of Britain's position on European security institutions in the early 1990s. The position was, and remains, a complex one, informed by more than one agenda. Several important steps were taken in Whitehall without which recent agreements might never have come about. But at the same time, there was ample evidence of the force of the political, institutional and military convictions outlined above.

Founded in October 1991 in response to NATO's establishment of a Rapid Reaction Corps under SACEUR, the Eurocorps was not received with composure in London and Washington, where the term 'Franco-German corps' was initially used in preference. In spite of the undoubted good intentions of the French and Germans, the concern was that the Eurocorps might divide the transatlantic security partnership at its most central, vital point: namely, US–European military cooperation under a single, unified NATO command structure. The compromise formula proposed by Malcolm Rifkind, then Britain's Secretary of State for Defence, in a speech in London in May 1992, was for the Eurocorps to be included among 'the forces made available to the WEU'. The WEU Council of Ministers, working to plans prepared by a WEU Planning Cell, would be able to deploy forces such as the Eurocorps, the UK–Netherlands Amphibious Force and even the air-mobile multinational division of the ARRC. But, tellingly, Rifkind could conceive of WEU-inspired and controlled operations only in situations 'when NATO chose not be engaged, for instance in humanitarian operations'.[21] At about this time, Britain was also assisting in the move of the WEU secretariat from London to Brussels, a gesture which was presented as proof of Britain's *bona fides* regarding the WEU and European security and defence cooperation.

The beginning of 1994 saw speculation begin to mount regarding Britain's intentions towards Europe. Following the NATO summit meeting in Brussels, an unprecedented trilateral meeting took place in London on 26 January between Rifkind, François Léotard and Volker Rühe (British, French and German defence ministers respectively). The purpose of the meeting was to discuss European defence cooperation in the light of the Brussels Summit and the launch of the CJTF idea. But with the French and Germans having agreed in January 1993 to place the Eurocorps under SACEUR's operational command in time of conflict, and with Belgium and Spain having joined the Franco-German initiative, Britain was also anxious to ensure it was not 'left on the sidelines' as the initiative gained momentum and respectability.[22] The meeting was reported as firm evidence of a 'distinct shift in the [British] government's view of European defense initiatives, and as underlining its anxiety to play a central role in European defense plans'. Furthermore, the meeting showed that Britain was now 'eager' to join France and Germany in developing the WEU as 'the European Union's defense wing'.[23] By autumn 1994 the British position was being reported boldly as a 'change of tack'. Following the publication by Rifkind of 'a secret paper recommending a more explicit European defence policy' in the summer, Britain was reported to be in favour of a *strengthened* west European defence and security identity, albeit one still firmly compatible with NATO.[24]

The latest phase in the evolution of British policy towards European security and defence cooperation began with the March 1995 memorandum on the EU's forthcoming inter-governmental conference.[25] The memorandum wasted little time before insisting upon the 'over-riding continuing importance of NATO' and expressing the British government's 'firm view that European nations should develop arrangements for the future that will ensure that, consistent with our NATO obligations, Europe collectively is able to shoulder more effectively its share of the burden of promoting security and stability on the European continent, on its periphery and beyond'. In the British view, the reactivated WEU had always been intended to be a means to improve the European contribution to NATO's 'European pillar' (note that 'European pillar' and WEU were not synonymous) and thereby share the burden of security more fairly with the United States. The wording of the Maastricht Treaty demanded a more subtle formulation, and so Whitehall had come to accept the idea of a WEU with a 'dual capacity', able both to contribute to the European pillar of NATO and to serve as 'the defence component of the European Union'. The memorandum also insisted on NATO's exclusive role in collective defence (Article 5) tasks, and cautioned against the 'wasteful' creation of new institutions. The United States was committed to Europe and would not remove its troops, 'unless forced to do so by its European allies'. Defence cooperation within Europe, in whatever forum, should be inter-governmental, and on no account should the WEU be folded into the EU.

In many respects, therefore, the memorandum was simply a restatement of established British views. However, it made an important and novel contribution in the form of an idea – 'task-based planning' – which could not only underpin all these faithful old assumptions, but could also form a basis for a Euro-Atlantic compromise. The document described a 'new strategic environment' in which military forces would be less likely to be used for traditional territorial defence operations, and more likely to find themselves involved in 'lesser crisis management tasks' such as peace support operations and humanitarian relief (the type of mission described in the WEU's June 1992 Petersberg Declaration). In order to fulfil these missions effectively, and in order to prevent non-membership of this or that institution from obstructing a state's will to join in the response to any such task, political and military flexibility would be essential. Institutional obsessiveness would be wholly out of place. NATO's core task of Article 5 collective defence would remain unchanged; but for the rest, it would be vital to be able to produce a rapid, operational response to inherently unpredictable crises and requirements, rather than rehearse the stale old institutional debate until it was too late to act. 'Task-based' military planning clearly complements the 'capability-based' military alliance discussed in chapter 2. In both cases, the attempt is made to give ad hoc cooperation some institutional flavour without removing too much flexibility and spontaneity. Finally, since task-based planning could, logically, as easily award 'lesser crisis management tasks' to NATO as to WEU, the new approach had no room for the NATO/WEU division of labour (except, of course, as far as collective defence was concerned). The memorandum stated firmly that 'we must avoid the trap of adopting simple assumptions – for example, that combat operations are for NATO and non-combat operations are for the WEU – which would place unnecessary constraints on the flexibility with which we can respond to the challenges we will face in the future.'

Within a matter of weeks, however, it was clear that the debate over the role of the WEU and the course and character of European defence and security cooperation was by no means resolved, and that the British compromise could not be accepted in many quarters. With Britain and several other WEU members 'adamant that any future security mechanisms complement NATO activities', the ministerial meeting of WEU members, associates, observers and associate partners in Lisbon in May 1995 'failed to mask differences over the future shape of European security' and 'revealed sharp differences over the effort to create a common European security architecture'.[26] In February 1996, following a meeting with Rühe in London, Britain's defence minister Michael Portillo verified that Britain would be willing to see 'Europe' carry out 'the "simpler military tasks" such as peace-keeping, guarding humanitarian aid and disaster relief on its own, and that this would gain favour in the US'.[27] Later the same month, the British Prime Minister John Major was to be heard denouncing the idea of 'endowing the EU with a military dimension by merging it gradually with the WEU'.[28] If there were still disagreements to be had between Britain and its European allies, it also became apparent that that the implications of the task-based planning approach had not been understood fully throughout Whitehall, particularly as regards the division of labour between institutions; the British foreign secretary's comments after the June 1996 Berlin agreement suggested the very same combat/non-combat distinction which had been made unfashionable by the task-based planning idea.

Britain's final contribution to the evolving discussion on European security institutions was made in March 1996, in a paper setting out the British government's negotiating agenda for the EU inter-governmental conference.[29] The paper confirmed all the trends outlined above; indeed, the entire March 1995 memorandum was included as an annex to the new paper. The British government's view of the character, object, form and instruments of European defence and security cooperation was comprehensively laid out. Any European cooperation should be a matter for governments; there should be no role for the European Commission, the European Parliament or the European Court of Justice. The object of any such cooperation should be to complement, rather than rival, NATO, which was 'the bedrock of European security'. Europeans could 'act on their own when necessary'; in the British view this meant dealing with smaller peacekeeping and humanitarian crises – if and when the United States and Canada chose not to participate. Britain remained averse to creating more institutions to serve this need; the WEU already provided 'the best framework for the further development of this [European] cooperation'. With its members, associate members, observers and associate partners, the WEU involved 27 west, central and east European states (agreement on Slovenia's associate partnership in June 1996 has since increased the number to 28). A 'reinforced partnership' between the two European institutions would mean the WEU could 'act on requests' from the EU, and would therefore complement 'the contribution that the EU can make to security with its own political and economic instruments'. Finally, the WEU would be able to 'draw on Alliance assets and facilities for use in European-led operations' through the developing CJTF scheme.

France and NATO

France's so-called *rapprochement* with NATO provides the third path to the June 1996 compromise at Berlin. For almost 30 years, since Charles de Gaulle withdrew France from the Alliance's integrated military structure in March 1966, ostensibly to pursue military self-sufficiency and an independent foreign policy, the relationship between NATO and France had been uncertain, and occasionally strained. In the French view, the end of the Cold War offered an opportunity to reorder European security institutions and remove several anomalies. The collapse of the Soviet threat would enable NATO's US-led integrated military structure to be reduced, if not dismantled entirely, and there would no longer be a requirement for the United States and NATO to be the focus of west European security concerns and institutions. At long last, France saw a real opportunity for west Europeans 'to construct a serious defence identity'.[30]

But in December 1995, following NATO's decision to send a 60,000-strong force to Bosnia-Herzegovina to replace UNPROFOR and the Anglo-French Rapid Reaction Force, the French defence minister Hervé de Charette announced his country's intention to develop a more constructive and open relationship with NATO. French chiefs of staff would take part in NATO's Military Committee, would improve their relations with the Alliance's military staff, and would work more closely with NATO's European command structure at SHAPE. The French defence minister would take part in all appropriate meetings with his NATO colleagues, but would not become a full, formal member of either the Defence Planning Committee or the Nuclear Planning Group (NPG). France would remain formally outside the Alliance's military structure. Full readmission to the Alliance and its military structure, including cooperation in nuclear planning, would not be contemplated, at least until France could be certain that NATO reform was 'under way and irreversible'.[31] The French change of approach was therefore conditional. It had also been carefully thought through.

The practical and intellectual basis for the French *rapprochement* with NATO had in fact been prepared long before the December 1995 announcements. The change of tack was the 'logical dénouement' of several years of improving relations between France and the Alliance.[32] France's participation in the US-led coalition against Iraq in 1990–1 was a salutary experience. A major contributor to the coalition, France nevertheless saw its forces operating 'parallel to but largely separate from' the main thrust of the effort. The operation against Iraq was run along NATO and SHAPE lines, and years of training in common procedures, liaison and interoperability were used to best effect. French equipment, communications and operating procedures were often found to be incompatible with NATO standards and practices, sometimes dangerously so. France also looked on with disappointment at the poor performance shown by European governments in former Yugoslavia, and became uncomfortably aware that the scope for European cooperation without some sort of US involvement might be much more limited than France had hoped and expected.

A more positive view of NATO had therefore begun to take hold even during the period of rivalry with the US in 1990 and 1991. In February 1991, in a move 'widely welcomed' by the Alliance,[33] France announced its decision to take part in NATO's Strategy Review Group (SRG), set up after the July 1990 London Declaration. From January 1993 French staff officers began to work closely with NATO's military planners on the implementation of a Bosnian peace settlement. Although France had left NATO's Military Committee in 1966, a military mission to the committee had been retained, albeit only with a 'consultative voice' appropriate to its observer status. In spring 1993 the head of France's mission was given 'deliberative' status as a participant in all Military Committee meetings when operations in former Yugoslavia, and peacekeeping in general, were being discussed.[34] Furthermore, where, for whatever reason, the existing International Military Staff (IMS) committee structure could not accommodate the French, ad hoc committees would often be created. In some cases these committees were given extraordinary privileges in being allowed to side-step the US-led military command structure and advise the NAC directly – a concession which would have been particularly welcomed in Paris. Following the January 1994 NATO summit in Brussels, French enthusiasm for NATO soared to new heights. A French official was reported as describing the summit as 'the best NATO summit ever, from France's viewpoint', and foreign minister Alain Juppé spoke warmly of a 'Franco-American entente' giving force and direction to the Alliance.[35]

The French *rapprochement* was a long-running as well as a changeable performance. Almost theatrically, each concession to NATO or the US–European defence and security partnership was followed by French assurances that they still had ideas of their own, were by no means returning contrite to the NATO family, and were not willing to accept all the Atlanticist rules, traditions and structures. Thus, in the same month in which it joined NATO's SRG, France united with Germany in presenting a paper to the European Community's Inter-Governmental Conference on Political Union (IGC (PU)). The paper stressed the need for a CFSP and called for the development of the WEU as the main source of European security. During 1991 and 1992 Pierre Joxe, French defence minister, called for improved relations between NATO and France; but then, at the Franco-German summit at La Rochelle in May 1992, Kohl and Mitterrand approved the further development of their October 1991 proposal for a Eurocorps. The delicate footwork continued even after the change of policy announced in December 1995. In March 1996 at Freiburg, France and Germany once again aired the idea of a 'European army', evidently not yet ready to accept one sceptical commentator's view that 'the idea of a joint defence is now slipping beyond the reach of the European Union'.[36] Later the same month Alain Juppé, by now the French prime minister, called for a 'European army numbering 350,000, independent of US control and answering to the European Union'. This force, made up of British, French, German,

Italian and Spanish troops, would be answerable in the first instance to the WEU, 'which itself would be subordinated to the European Union'.[37] And then, just days after the Berlin ministerial meeting, Kohl and Chirac met for the twice-yearly Franco-German summit in Dijon, vowing to 'raise the profile of the EU in foreign and security affairs'.[38]

Yet any vacillations in the new French view of NATO are more fairly described as cautious than capricious. Keen for domestic reasons to restructure its armed forces and reduce defence spending, by endorsing the Alliance's dynamic involvement in Bosnia, France had declared that the best hope for a well-organized, meaningful and above all cost-effective European security structure would lie, first and foremost, in NATO rather than in some exclusively European politico-military institution or formation. As far as engineering the Berlin compromise is concerned, the French *rapprochement* with NATO not only placed the Alliance at the centre of post-Cold War European defence and security, it also snubbed the 'Euro-integrationists' by stressing that any European cooperation in defence and security should be inter-governmental. The new French approach also endorsed the view that the connection with the United States was vital for European security, and that one object of European cooperation should be to prevent a slump in US morale over the burden-sharing issue. Given decades of Gaullist suspicion of NATO and all things American, and given France's earlier enthusiasm for a European solution to Europe's defence needs after the Cold War, the French change of direction was striking, and certainly electrified the Alliance.

France clearly did not see itself as the prodigal returning apologetically to the fold. Nor, clearly, was it doing cynically only what was necessary to contain or even derail the development of NATO after the Cold War. France now had a carefully considered view of the role of the United States and NATO in European defence and security after the Cold War. Yet this view, and the concessions it implied, were not to be taken for granted; France was offering to make a bargain with the Atlanticists, and there was a price to be paid for its contribution to any agreed institutional framework. One part of the price was the assurance that there would still be enough scope for genuine, European defence and security cooperation within NATO and the broader US–European partnership. The second part of the price – growing out of France's preference for inter-governmental cooperation in matters of defence as well as its insistence on the development of a discrete, competent European 'identity' – was acknowledgment that the US–European partnership should be just that, rather than something akin to the Cold War model of US military hegemony over western Europe generally and particularly within the Alliance's political and military decision-making structures. The 'new NATO', in the French view, should be one in which the military structures were fully accountable to, and controlled by, the political core of the Alliance (the NAC – which France had never left), and sufficiently flexible and decentralized to allow effective expression of the developing European security and defence identity. There is another, less magnanimous interpretation of French behaviour, which is that France, with an eye to a diminished US involvement in European security at some time in the future, was preparing itself 'systematically for a leading role in European defense'.[39]

The timing and style of the French change of direction also contributed procedurally to the June 1996 compromise. Beneath the rhetoric, the long-established military liaison between NATO and France was already, quite clearly, developing into a far more intimate relationship. But the steadily increasing French involvement had had a curiously inhibiting, if not destructive effect on NATO's deliberations during the early 1990s. In the words of one British military official; 'It was immediately obvious that the French military were keen to co-operate but were constantly given unhelpful instructions from Paris of a political nature to ensure that sufficient progress was made to prevent breakdown, but stopping short of decisions that would allow the Alliance to move ahead.'[40] With no vote, France had no real power to halt progress, and could therefore easily be overridden at the Military Committee. But an enlightened, rather than confrontational, view prevailed; whatever the long-term future of the Alliance and the US–European security partnership, it was difficult to see how or on what grounds France could be excluded from it. The British in particular argued for an inclusive approach towards their erstwhile Europeanist 'adversary', even at the price of holding up committee business. In a sense, therefore, rather than initiating a whole new process of debate and discussion, the French moves in late 1995 released a logjam, with disproportionate effect. The official momentum needed for the Berlin agreement did not have to be manufactured carefully and slowly – it appeared almost overnight.

Germany – lubricating the transatlantic security partnership

Since the late 1940s the Western allies have sought to construct and maintain a politico-military framework which could, at once, restrain or contain the Federal Republic's potential, accommodate its wishes and priorities as an ally, physically protect its territory and interests, and exploit its economic and military strength for alliance purposes. The launch of the WEU in 1954–5 was, largely, a device to enable controlled, 'Europeanized' West German rearmament and membership of NATO. Similarly, NATO's development of the strategies of forward defence and flexible response in the 1960s and 1970s were the Alliance's response to Germany's 'special needs'.

For its part, Germany has shaped its security and defence thinking around a set of ideological and practical imperatives.[41] First, Germany has positioned itself at the centre of the movement towards 'ever closer' economic and political union in western Europe, both as a leading proponent of the idea and, with its recent history in mind, as an illustration of the perils of failure in the great enterprise. The view of the long-serving Chancellor Helmut Kohl and his party, the CDU, is that closer political union should, in time, encompass foreign, security and defence policies. This is the principal distinction between German and British views, which are otherwise close. Second, Germany has developed a close relationship with France in all areas of policy, and has been content to see the Franco-German relationship become the main force behind the postwar west European security community. In terms of defence and military security, Germany has pursued a 'special relationship' with France since the signature of the Elysée Treaty in January 1963. Third, Germany has sought to maintain US commitment to European security under the auspices of NATO. By one account, Germany's relationship with the United States is 'perhaps the closest of all the NATO allies'.[42]

Each of these imperatives has pulled Germany in a different direction, although the first two have overlapped reasonably well. In the great, European scheme of things, the need to sustain US defence cooperation always sat somewhat awkwardly, but during the Cold War its importance was undeniable. After the Cold War, Germany was forced to find a more convincing and coherent formula to avoid competing loyalties. Close relations with France seemed a relatively straightforward part of the formula (at least until early 1996). In January 1988, the French and Germans marked the twenty-fifth anniversary of the Elysée Treaty with an additional protocol establishing a Joint Defence and Security Council. The 4,000-strong Franco-German brigade was created in the same year. Ministerial, military and defence-industrial relations between the two countries were reinforced in the early 1990s. Germany had more difficulty, however, in reconciling its Europeanist idealism with its Atlanticist pragmatism. The way out of this dilemma was to present European security and defence cooperation (and even integration) as a medium- or long-term (rather than immediate) goal, which would complement and strengthen, rather than undermine, the crucial Atlantic partnership, and which would not involve any additional cost. European security could best be assured through a more balanced transatlantic partnership between the North American allies on the one hand, and a more cohesive and efficient NATO–European bloc on the other.[43] Simply put, Germany sought a formula which could enable it to be *both* Europeanist/idealist *and* Atlanticist/pragmatist, rather than be forced into choosing one or the other combination.

Consistent with its reputation as a committed 'good European', Germany might have been expected to see the collapse of the Soviet military threat as an opportunity to progress to a fully mature union in post-Cold War Europe, with competence and autonomy in foreign, security and even defence policies. Certainly, there were several occasions in the early 1990s when Germany's intention appeared to be to 'Europeanize' European security, even at the expense of the Atlantic partnership. In December 1990 Kohl and Mitterrand wrote to their European Council colleagues to suggest that the WEU be placed at the centre of the debate on European security institutions. The letter was met with a 'stern *démarche*' from Washington, resulting in a statement from the German and French foreign ministers (Genscher and Dumas) to the effect that the WEU should be subordinated to NATO.[44] Any contrition in Paris and Bonn did not endure for long, however. In February 1991 the Franco-German proposals to the IGC (PU) on political union called again for the elevation of the WEU at the expense of NATO, eliciting an Anglo-Italian counter-attack later in the year. Undeterred, Kohl and Mitterrand fought back with a proposal to expand their combined brigade into a full army corps which other WEU members could join in time. In Britain and the United States, the development of the Eurocorps from late 1991 was widely seen as an unabashed attempt to undermine NATO.[45] After painstaking negotiation over the role of the Eurocorps in the overall European security picture, the new formation was declared operational on 30 November 1995.

The resolution of the Eurocorps issue seemed briefly to indicate some moderation in Bonn's Euro-enthusiasm. In February 1996, during a meeting in London with Portillo, Rühe reportedly 'ruled out the idea of a European army', arguing that 'It must be a coalition of the able and willing ... You can't by a majority decision decide to send somebody else's soldiers into battle.'[46] Yet by other accounts Kohl still clung to the idea of a European army of some sort, to the possibility of a medium-term future merger of the EU and the WEU, and even to the possibility of making security and defence decisions by majority vote. Germany's dogged adherence to the goal (however distant) of European defence autonomy continued to be frowned upon in Britain. France also reacted less than enthusiastically, particularly (albeit *sotto voce*) to Germany's ostensible desire to extend majority voting into matters of defence and security.[47] With France reacting almost as a senior colleague embarrassed by its ingenuous and over-zealous junior, an intriguing interpretation begins to emerge of Germany's management of its security relationship with France.

Germany has usually taken pains to present its Europeanist goals as being at least consistent with – if not a positive support for – a broadly traditional, Atlanticist approach to the question of European defence and security. At the June 1996 NATO meeting in Berlin, Germany and France reiterated their by now familiar position on the merger of the EU and WEU. But at the Berlin meeting Germany was also 'particularly anxious that ammunition should not be given to US congressmen who want to withdraw the remaining 100,000 troops from Europe'.[48] Two explanations are usually offered for Germany's reluctance to renounce NATO in the post-Cold War scramble to devise a new 'architecture' for European security: culture and cost. The first is that, for cultural and historical reasons, Germany has been – and remains – as keen as its allies in wishing to integrate its armed forces into a close-knit, well-organized multilateral politico-military framework. In the German view, NATO is unrivalled in this respect. NATO would have to adapt and remain dynamic in order to ensure that it, and not some rival institution, would be entrusted with the vital task of restraining Germany into the next century.[49] The second explanation lies in the impossibility of financing a credible alternative to NATO.

All NATO allies have faced growing pressure for retrenchment in defence spending after the Cold War. But Bonn has been confronted with the greater and more urgent problem of German unification and has had to find over DM900 billion – through 'solidarity' taxes and other devices – with which to modernize industry and infrastructure in the former Democratic Republic and support its fragile economy. Germany is also burdened with the largest contribution (about 30 per cent) to the EU budget, and is keen to shape its economy to fulfil the convergence criteria for entry into the anticipated economic and monetary union. Given all these circumstances, Germany's armed forces have come to be seen as 'the main savings source for the federal government'.[50] The prospect of deep defence cuts by Germany at first filled the Americans with alarm. Yet, as expressed by Rühe in November 1996, the good husbandry demanded by Germany's straitened financial circumstances would lead to a situation with which both NATO and the United States could be content: 'The very fact that we have achieved consensus on creating a European capability for acting within the framework of the Alliance is a political success in itself, *since we are avoiding duplication of structures and waste of resources.*'[51]

Germany's more ambitious Europeanism may have reflected the need to establish a negotiating position for the 1996–7 EU IGC. It is also conceivable that Bonn saw that it would be considered – domestically and by its allies – inappropriate for Germany either to question the EU orthodoxy and the Franco-German relationship which lay beneath it or to become too vocal a proponent of the reform and adaptation of the world's most efficient and potent military organization – NATO. The 'intriguing interpretation' mentioned above, although based on no more than circumstantial evidence, now begins to take clearer shape. Could it be argued that Germany's Europeanist, integrationist rhetoric was an affectation which could only be indulged during the Cold War, when no real threat to the primacy of NATO and US cooperation could seriously have been entertained? And with the end of the Cold War, rather than renouncing its idealism as inimical to the cause of sustaining the transatlantic connection, could Germany have seen a new, more practical application for its rhetoric?

Conventional wisdom has it that when France announced major reforms to its military structure and defence industry in February 1996, Germany was dismayed, offended and even 'livid' at not having been briefed in advance.[52] The plot may be thicker, however, and even a little Machiavellian. Rather than merely helping France towards its *rapprochement* with NATO and the United States,[53] Germany may have structured the debate so as to give France no real alternative, and thereby overcome France's 'disappointment' with Germany's finance-driven reluctance to consider a real alternative to NATO.[54] Germany's two major European allies have each offered a different solution to the European security problem. While both Britain and France have favoured inter-governmentalism, the former has married it to Atlanticism, and the latter to Europeanism. Faced with these alternatives, Germany may have

51

artfully pursued a third course – Europeanism with integrationism. This would provide Germany with its *bona fides* as a committed European, but would also outmanoeuvre the French and steer them towards the Atlanticism which Germany has always, at bottom, considered so vital. By associating Europeanism with integrationism, Germany may have hoped that France would find Europeanism indigestible, prompting it to satisfy its other main desideratum – inter-governmentalism – through an Atlantic association. If the Franco-German security relationship were to be undermined or modified in some major way, and if France and Germany were even slightly to become estranged, what better result for Germany than that it should improve France's view of NATO and the United States' view of its military involvement in Europe?

Conclusion   *eg eurocorps*

By early 1996, policy shifts in the United States, Britain and France had created a more consensual atmosphere regarding the characteristics and purpose of European defence and security cooperation after the Cold War. This new atmosphere was not especially rich, and could not support all forms of life, but neither was it sterile. Broad agreement could be found on five key features of a post-Cold War European security framework:

give examples of those

- cooperation in matters of defence and security should – at least for the present – be inter-governmental;
- the US commitment to European defence and security should be preserved;
- NATO should remain at the heart of European defence and security;
- defence and security cooperation by European allies should complement, rather than rival, NATO and the broader transatlantic partnership;
- The WEU could act as a general lubricant in preserving the partnership and ensuring its smooth running.

Many important issues remained to be resolved: institutional reform of NATO; the degree of political and operational (i.e. military) autonomy which ESDI would have within NATO; and the possibility of a future merger between the WEU and the EU. But by mid-1996 the four most important architects of post-Cold War transatlantic security had clearly reached a level of consensus. Without this consensus it is unlikely that the compromise engineered in June 1996 and developed thereafter could ever have emerged, and it is to that compromise that we now turn.

Chapter 4

Military adaptation: NATO's twenty-first-century triad

Introduction

Having shown how US, British, French and German policies coalesced to create an atmosphere in which compromise could be reached, the task of this chapter, and the succeeding one, is to describe the outcome for the Euro-Atlantic defence and security partnership. It is tempting to see the June 1996 NAC ministerial in Berlin as the culmination of this process. But it is important to remember both that the compromise had taken several years to evolve and that the Berlin meeting raised many more questions than could be answered immediately. The meeting was followed by months of detailed planning work by NATO's political and military committees, working initially to a December 1996 deadline, but latterly with a view to completing the adaptation process by the July 1997 NATO summit meeting. The July 1997 deadline itself subsequently slipped to December 1997. The development of a 'new' defence and security structure for Europe has been a steady and evolutionary process, and one which is by no means concluded.

Using the Berlin NAC meeting as a dividing line, this chapter traces the course of NATO's internal adaptation, up to NATO's Summit for Euro-Atlantic Cooperation and Security held in Madrid on 8–9 July 1997. Adaptation can be divided into three closely related areas: overall strategy, command structure and force posture (including the development of the CJTF concept). The first part of the chapter examines developments made in each of these areas between the July 1990 NATO summit meeting in London and the Berlin ministerial almost six years later. The second part of the chapter addresses the same three areas, albeit in a different order. Particular attention is paid to the Alliance's command and control structure and its force posture, important modifications to which were set in train at the June 1996 Berlin NAC meeting, but were still being debated well into 1997. At the Madrid Summit NATO's 1991 Strategic Concept, having for some years been a relatively stable feature of the adaptation process, was also brought into the post-Berlin review process; it is discussed in the final part of the chapter.

NATO adaptation: the London Declaration, July 1990

At their summit meeting in London in July 1990, Alliance leaders acknowledged recent changes in Europe and stated plainly that, 'as a consequence, this Alliance must and will adapt.'[1] The London Declaration set the tone for subsequent change in the Alliance. Adaptation would be both political and military. In the name of political adaptation, Article 2 of the North Atlantic Treaty would be re-emphasized to promote 'stability', 'well-being' and 'economic collaboration' among the allies, and the Declaration welcomed the development of 'a European identity in the domain of security'. NATO would also 'reach out' and extend 'the hand of friendship' to former Warsaw Pact adversaries. In time, 'reaching out' to eastern Europe would develop into the NACC (and latterly the EAPC), the PfP programme and the enlargement programme.

Military adaptation would address the Alliance's force structure and strategy, and to that end the London Declaration set out three objectives, the first of which could almost be an early draft of the CJTF concept:

> NATO will field smaller and restructured active forces. These forces will be highly mobile and versatile so that Allied leaders will have maximum flexibility in deciding how to respond to a crisis. It will rely increasingly on multinational corps made up of national units.

The second objective was a response to the need for retrenchment after the Cold War:

> NATO will scale back the readiness of its active units, reducing training requirements and the number of exercises.

Finally, the third objective made it clear that in all the euphoria following the destruction of the Berlin Wall, NATO had not forgotten about the core Article 5 task of collective self-defence:

NATO will rely more heavily on the ability to build up larger forces if and when they might be needed.[2]

To meet these objectives, NATO would require a new strategic framework and rationale, a flexible command structure capable of imaginative and dynamic contingency planning, and a force structure which could offer high-readiness, highly capable forces able to cover a range of contingencies from small, short-warning operations to full-scale collective defence.

Strategy review

Within the NATO and SHAPE bureaucracies (civilian and military), a common reaction to the cataclysmic events of 1989 was to assume that NATO's 22-year-old Overall Strategic Concept for the Defence of the NATO Area – otherwise known as MC 14-3, with its twin pillars of 'forward defence' and 'flexible response' – would somehow manage to keep pace with change.[3] There may have been a certain amount of bureaucratic discomfort, therefore, when NATO's defence ministers decided, early in 1990, completely to review the Alliance's military strategy and the operational plans and doctrines which flowed from it.[4] The London Declaration confirmed this decision and spoke of replacing 'forward defence' with 'reduced forward presence', of modifying the 'flexible response' strategy and of developing 'new force plans consistent with the revolutionary changes in Europe'.[5] NATO could not, however, bring itself to renounce its long-standing insistence on the right to initiate use of nuclear weapons. The Alliance's doctrine of 'no no-first-use' – and nuclear strategic issues generally – were to figure prominently in subsequent outreach and enlargement discussions.

The review of NATO's strategy was carried out from July 1990 by an Ad Hoc Group on the Legge Review of NATO's Military Strategy, otherwise known as the SRG or Legge Group, after its chairman Michael Legge. It had taken seven years for MC14-3 to emerge; the review lasted just 16 months, with much of the substantive work completed in the first two or three. Following the May 1991 announcement by the DPC of a new force structure,[6] the NAC decision in June to establish the ARRC and the July 1991 Copenhagen NAC Declaration setting out the Alliance's four 'core security functions',[7] the scene was set for the November 1991 launch, at the Rome Summit, of the Alliance's new Strategic Concept.[8]

By the time of the Rome Summit, Alliance governments had accepted that the task of collective defence was no longer urgent, and was no longer a sufficient rationale for the Alliance. In addition, NATO would henceforth have to manage 'more diverse tasks' such as intra-state conflict.[9] To carry out old and new missions, the Strategic Concept called for a force posture which could enable the Alliance to respond across the military spectrum, from 'managing crises that affect the security of the Alliance members' to the 'unlikely' possibility of a 'major conflict'. This multi-role force posture would integrate sea, land and air power into dynamic arrangements which could 'build up, deploy and draw down forces quickly and discriminately' and allow 'flexible and timely responses in order to reduce and defuse tensions'. Multinational cooperation was a vital ingredient, to underwrite the credibility both of the Alliance and of its collective defence strategy. Multinational forces – particularly the immediate and rapid reaction forces – would 'reinforce solidarity' and would enable a more precise and efficient use of dwindling defence resources.[10]

Even a passing survey of the Strategic Concept reveals two things. First, much of the language, and many of the ideas, which were later to propel the CJTF into the limelight were clearly present in these early stages and were at the centre of NATO's efforts to restructure itself politically and militarily. Second, the object of this restructuring was to produce *one* force posture which could satisfy *both* the traditional collective defence function and the new 'non-Article 5' tasks. General John Galvin, SACEUR at the time of the Rome Summit, gave a succinct account of what had been agreed: 'Our military forces will be capable of several missions, including deterrence and support for crisis management, peace-keeping, humanitarian assistance, and, as before, the defence of Alliance territory.'[11]

Before examining the force posture review and the development of the CJTF idea, adaptation of NATO's command structure after the Cold War should first be taken into account.

Command structure review

The end of the Cold War in 1989 found NATO with a 'strategic area' divided into three Major NATO Commands (MNCs): Allied Command Atlantic (ACLANT), Allied Command Europe (ACE) and Allied Command Channel (ACCHAN). The North American area was covered by a US–Canadian Regional Planning Group, a legacy from the pre-Korean War days of NATO military planning. The three MNCs, commanded respectively by SACLANT, SACEUR and CINCCHAN, were geographically and functionally responsible for NATO defence in their areas, including defence plans, force requirements, deployments, exercises and training. The MNCs took instructions from the Military Committee (MC) which in turn was subordinate to the North Atlantic Council (NAC) and the Defence Planning Committee (DPC). Beneath each MNC was a layer of Major Subordinate Commands (MSC); SACEUR, for example, could call on Commander-in-Chief Allied Forces Northern Europe (CINCNORTH), his colleague in the central region (CINCENT) and in the south (CINCSOUTH). And beneath each MSC lay a whole raft of Principal Subordinate Commands (PSCs) and sub-PSCs, covering a variety of territorial responsibilities and functional tasks. When France withdrew from NATO's integrated military structure in 1966, it ceased to offer military formations to the regional commands and lost its representation on the MC and the DPC. Although France retained its 'political' seat on the NAC, this founding body of the Alliance was (until 13 June 1996) at one remove from what France saw as the all-important DPC-MC politico-military nexus, into which France no longer had any direct, formal input.

By the end of the Cold War, NATO was therefore the proud owner of an integrated military command structure which, however well it may have worked in the past, was widely perceived to be too vast, complex and expensive. It was also a structure designed primarily to respond to Warsaw Pact aggression in Europe. Cold War NATO planning assumed that the main battle would take place in the 'Central Region' of Europe along the former inner-German border, with aggression also expected on the 'flanks'. An elaborate 'General Defence Plan' (GDP) was drawn up to absorb, delay and eventually repulse aggression in Europe, and it was around the execution, reinforcement and support of this plan that the whole of NATO's military structure revolved. But it became clear that, with the collapse of the Soviet Union and the Warsaw Treaty Organization, neither the GDP nor its courtiers had any clothes. Thus, alongside strategy, the size and efficiency of NATO's Cold War command structure formed the second element of the Alliance's overall review. As the security risks and challenges facing the Alliance became increasingly diffuse and unpredictable, so it became all the more important to ensure that the command structure was healthy and adaptable: 'Without a well-structured, discrete, unambiguous chain of command, from the highest political levels to the troops in the field, no military organization will perform to the optimum, however well equipped, motivated and trained. This is particularly true in a multinational environment.'[12] And, it might be added, particularly true in the absence of an unambiguous general threat.

After the July 1990 London Declaration, a high-level working group was created to examine NATO's command structure and suggest improvements. The group was to work within the following criteria:

- any revisions to the Alliance's command structure would have to ensure the timely flow of military advice to political authorities, as well as political guidance to the military;
- a revised command structure would have to ensure continued US and Canadian involvement in collective defence and security planning;
- a revised structure should be flexible enough to allow for a European security and defence identity.[13]

The working group examined the existing division of the NATO area into MNCs and considered three main options:

- maintain and adapt the existing arrangement;
- substitute one Atlantic MNC and two European MNCs (northern and southern regions);
- substitute one Atlantic MNC, one European MNC and a functional MNC responsible for nuclear matters, rapid reaction and certain other strategic matters.[14]

The second option was rejected on the grounds that it would divide the European theatre and thereby undermine the principle of unity of command. The third option, with a combination of geographical and functional MNCs, was also rejected as being unnecessarily complicated. This left the first option – adaptation of the existing structure.

Within the first model, a reduction to two MNCs was considered, along two different lines. The first would see a functional division between a European air/land MNC and a NATO-wide maritime MNC; this was thought to present too many coordination problems for the wider NATO area. The second option would see one MNC for continental Europe and another for the Atlantic. The drawback with this option was that European command representation might be too limited if there were only two MNCs, whereas adequate European representation could be assumed if the existing three-MNC structure was maintained. The working group could reach no solution and passed the problem 'upstairs' to the Military Committee. To find a way out of the imbroglio, a Four Nation Working Group (Britain, Denmark, Germany and Norway) was established to consider the options and make a decision. In the end, this group recommended a two-MNC structure.

The ministerial session of the DPC on 12–13 December 1991 accepted the recommended reduction of NATO's MNCs from three to two (SACEUR and SACLANT), with the abolition of the Channel Command. Within ACE, the DPC also accepted the recommended reorganization around three MSCs: AFSOUTH, AFCENT and the new AFNORTHWEST. But with ACLANT retaining five MSCs, NATO's command structure would still be very rich in generals and admirals. The coruscation was even more apparent at the PSC level; two of ACE's MSCs (AFNORTHWEST and AFCENT) would each retain three PSCs, each commanded by a 'three star' (lieutenant general or equivalent) or 'four star' (general or equivalent) officer. Each of these commanders would have a headquarters with staffs for operational, intelligence and logistic planning. The inevitable, awkward question was asked by one senior British official late in 1992: 'What will all these people do?' This stage of the rationalization of the command structure was finally accepted by NATO defence ministers in May 1992, when changes to the PSC structure were also approved. Economy and efficiency provided a powerful rationale for retrenchment; the DPC expected manpower savings of as much as 20 per cent as a result of reductions in the number and size of NATO headquarters.[15]

The pace of reform in the command structure slowed in 1993 when the DPC decided to allow the changes made so far to consolidate, and to allow other working groups and committees to take account of command structure changes. By this stage in the process there was wide agreement that the number of headquarters should be reduced, perhaps by removing one whole layer of the command structure. But there was little if any willingness among NATO members to give up any NATO headquarters stationed on their territory. 'Ownership' of a NATO headquarters brought with it influence and prestige in NATO, for the commander and for his country, as well as local economic and infrastructure benefits. At about this time the fate of ACLANT was also being discussed; given that ACLANT was increasingly being seen as a provider of support to ACE, would it be possible for NATO to have just one MNC (SACEUR) with SACLANT reduced to MSC status? This proposal failed to gather much support, not least because to have downgraded ACLANT – the only major NATO headquarters on US soil – would have been a 'major snub' to the United States.[16]

The January 1994 NATO summit declaration called for further adaptation of the command system. On 1 June 1994 the long-awaited reduction in MNCs took place when the decision to disband ACCHAN was put into effect. ACE and ACLANT remained, both MNCs to be commanded by American officers. The functions and assets of the Channel Command were transferred to ACE. Within ACE, the earlier recommendation for a three-way division between MSCs AFNORTHWEST (British commander), AFCENT (German commander) and AFSOUTH (US commander) was also implemented.

At their ministerial session in spring 1995, NATO defence ministers agreed to launch the next stage of the command review and consolidation process, in the form of a Long Term Study carried out by the MC and scheduled for completion by autumn 1996.[17] One purpose of the Long Term Study was to decide whether a quantitative approach to the command review was sufficient or whether, instead, a complete qualitative revision should take place. During the Cold War the upper echelons of NATO's command structure had combined geographical and functional responsibilities; only at the lower levels did a separation between the two become apparent. The question the Long Term Study was to examine was whether geographical divisions could be appropriate at *any* level of the command structure, or whether a more flexible, functional multinational command structure should replace the MSC level.[18]

With the survival of the two MNCs – ACE and ACLANT – assured, the fate of the MSCs and PSCs now became the real source of controversy. Within ACLANT, it was proposed that the MSCs be reduced from three to two: EASTLANT (with a British commander) and WESTLANT (with a US commander). The discontinued MSC would be IBERLANT. But IBERLANT was a Portuguese 'owned' command, and Lisbon was predictably unwilling to accept its demise. Within ACE the debate revolved around whether, having cut UKAIR to reduce the number of MSCs to three (AFNORTHWEST, AFCENT and AFSOUTH), any further reduction could be contemplated. Especially bitter arguments blew up when reform of the PSC and sub-PSC levels was considered. The threatened removal of a PSC was generally perceived in strategic, political and economic terms as a loss of security, prestige and income; and the decision to shift the funding of sub-PSC headquarters from NATO to host governments only added to the national cost of NATO restructuring.

By the time of the Berlin ministerial the allies had clearly taken important steps in reorganizing and streamlining NATO's command structure. But there were still a number of fundamental disagreements. The object of the command structure review had been to introduce the principles of flexibility, rapid reaction, joint deployment and multinational cooperation into every layer of the command structure. But alongside the unexceptional goals of making the command structure more streamlined, efficient and adaptable, the command review was also intended to provide 'workable interfaces between NATO and the evolving plans for European defence contributions under [WEU] ... Effective practical mechanisms will be needed to ensure compatibility between the respective NATO and European defence organizations, and to avoid confusion or unnecessary duplication.'[19] In other words, the adaptation of NATO's command structure was determined not merely by the need to reflect the outcome of the strategy and force posture reviews which were taking place in parallel, but also by the need to satisfy demands for a more 'European' flavour to the Alliance and the way it conducts its business. It was for this reason that so much attention was paid to the MSC level, particularly within ACE, since it would be here that the CJTF concept – when it had a predominantly land force component and in its role as a bridge to ESDI – would succeed or fail. One especially difficult question was whether ESDI's mid-level entry-point into the Alliance's command structure would be acceptable to all involved, or whether there would be calls for greater ESDI 'visibility' at the level of the MNCs, which were destined to be US-led.

Force posture review

The adaptation of NATO's force posture also had quantitative and qualitative dimensions. The first was essentially a matter of imposing some sense of order and control upon national military retrenchment. The second was a case of ensuring that the forces which remained would be susceptible to collective organization and capable of carrying out the new, more diverse and open-ended strategy agreed in 1991. NATO's force reduction was implemented after 1993. Set against the figures for 1990, the overall planned peacetime strength of the Alliance would be reduced by as much as 25 per cent in some functions. As far as ground forces were concerned, the total number of combat units would be reduced by 25 per cent, and the total peacetime strength of land forces in NATO's Central Region (i.e. those forces prepared to carry out the Cold War GDP) would be reduced by 45 per cent. NATO's naval forces would be reduced by 10 per cent. The total number of NATO comb at aircraft stationed in Europe would also be reduced by over 25 per cent, with the Central and Northern regions of ACE being affected disproportionately.[20]

Deliberations on the qualitative dimension resulted in the three-level force structure agreed at Rome in 1991. Reaction Forces would consist of mobile and highly capable land, sea and air forces. Reaction forces at the highest state of readiness (available for deployment within days) would be known as the Immediate Reaction Force, with larger, formation-level components providing the Rapid Reaction Force. 'Rapid reaction' was interpreted by the first commander of the ARRC as requiring the lead elements of his command to be ready to move within seven days, and the remainder within 15 days.[21] The Main Defence Forces would account for the greater part of the new force structure, and would include 'active and mobilisable ground, air and maritime forces able to deter and defend against coercion or aggression'.[22] Forces in this category – including the Eurocorps when assigned to NATO – would also be available for crisis management operations. Finally, Augmentation Forces would include all other NATO-assigned forces which, although under strength or requiring further training before deployment, could be used to reinforce a NATO operation if the need arose.

Qualitative restructuring saw an emphasis on flexibility and mobility of forces, reflecting the military instinct to 'expect the unexpected' as well as the likelihood that the fewer forces available would have to be spread more thinly. This emphasis can be seen both in the two-level Reaction Forces and in the development of the CJTF concept.

The idea of the CJTF was first floated by the Americans in 1993 and endorsed in January 1994 at the NATO summit meeting in Brussels. The summit declaration set out several key functions of the Alliance, to each of which the CJTF concept could make a contribution:

- to maintain the transatlantic partnership – 'the bedrock of NATO' (para. 2);
- to give substance to ESDI, the 'European pillar' of the Alliance, by enabling the use of collective NATO assets in European/ WEU-led operations (paras 6 and 8);
- to enable flexible and timely response by NATO to a broad range of traditional and new security risks and challenges (paras 7 and 8);
- to support UN- or CSCE-sponsored 'peacekeeping and other operations', on the basis of coalitions of the willing (para. 7);
- in parallel with the PfP programme, to enhance the prospects for cooperation with non-NATO countries (paras 8 and 9).[23]

Following the January summit, a SHAPE report on CJTF was completed in April 1994. At this stage, CJTF was seen as a relatively simple matter of introducing a detachable element at existing NATO headquarters. A CJTF headquarters, with its own staff, command and control and logistics support, would be detached from the NATO command structure and established in a conflict area beyond NATO's borders, where it would command forces up to army corps or equivalent. The development and 'Europeanization' of the CJTF idea stalled during 1994 when France became uneasy about the proximity of CJTF to the integrated command structure.[24] But during 1995 and 1996 the principal features of the CJTF idea became clearer. Six particular observations may be made.

First, the model of military cooperation encapsulated in the CJTF idea is by no means a new one. On 13 June 1996 a milestone was reached in NATO's development after the Cold War when, for the first time in 30 years, NATO's defence ministers met at the level of the NAC. Furthermore, in an important concession to the French, the meeting was 'at sixteen', i.e., with the full and formal participation of France's defence minister.[25] The NAC/DM communiqué defined CJTF as 'multinational and multiservice formations established for specific contingency operations'.[26] Throughout history, whenever powers have cooperated militarily, formations of this sort have been standard military practice. Nationally, the concept of a joint task force is very well established, with the United States in particular being very interested in pursuing the idea.[27] The potential of a *combined* JTF became apparent in 1992 when NATO's decommissioned Northern Army Group headquarters (previously a PSC under AFCENT) was moved from its base in Germany to Bosnia-Herzegovina to run peace support operations there. But cooperative task forces have not usually been known for their longevity: 'CJTFs are situation-specific. By their very nature, joint task forces have limited life spans – dictated by the contingency they are developed to address.'[28] What was unusual – indeed, 'unprecedented in military doctrine' – about the CJTF idea was that it would 'institutionalise the task force concept, a command and control arrangement normally employed for crisis response by ad hoc coalitions'.[29]

Second, it has become clear that NATO has firm ambitions to be a crisis manager and peacekeeper in its own right, with the appropriate UN or OSCE mandate, and that CJTF will be a means to achieve that goal. As noted earlier, forerunners of the CJTF concept had suggested a division of labour between NATO and the WEU, with the former responsible for

Article 5 collective defence and the latter for lower-scale, non-Article 5 missions. But NATO quickly became uncomfortable with this prospect – known as 'bifurcation' – and argued that it, too, should have some means to carry out non-Article 5 missions, not least because international legitimation and public approval were more readily available for such missions than for full-scale, collective defence against some notional threat. Another criticism of a NATO/WEU division of labour was that it offered little or no room to discuss whether or not the United States (and Canada) should take part in a given non-Article 5 operation. Thus, in its Oslo communiqué of 4 June 1992 and on many other occasions, the NAC tried to position NATO as a crisis manager on behalf of the CSCE, rejecting any neat division of labour between NATO and the WEU. In September 1993 at the IISS in London, NATO's Secretary-General Manfred Wörner destroyed any remaining illusions by declaring that non-Article 5 missions were not the exclusive preserve of the WEU.[30] So, whatever the original design and whatever other jobs it may have been awarded along the way, by June 1996 CJTF had become unequivocally a mechanism for NATO peacekeeping and crisis management. If there was to be a NATO/WEU division of labour, it could only be *within* the non-Article 5 category, with NATO taking 'hard' missions with fighting potential and the WEU dealing with 'soft' humanitarian and rescue missions. The 13 June 1996 NAC/defence ministerial communiqué showed precisely where NATO's priorities lay in setting up the CJTF scheme: 'an exercise should be conducted as soon as practicable, based on the deployment of a CJTF *for a NATO-led contingency operation*. We also invite the WEU to work with NATO on the preparation for a *subsequent* CJTF exercise based on a WEU-led operation.'[31]

The third observation to be made here is that CJTF is not simply a Euro-friendly afterthought in NATO's restructuring process, but lies at the heart of that process. One US analyst saw the CJTF as a 'logical outgrowth of the new strategic concept' in so far as it would give NATO much-needed flexibility and mobility across the spectrum of possible conflict.[32] Shortly after the January 1994 Brussels Summit the concept was described by NATO's Secretary-General as 'the next logical step in [the] adaptation of our force structures'.[33] CJTF would be an omnibus arrangement, able to provide an appropriate response across the spectrum of possible military tasks, ranging from the admittedly unlikely collective defence to non-Article 5 crises and missions. To achieve the goal of 'one system capable of performing multiple functions', avoiding wasteful duplication of forces and command structures, the vital ingredients would be mobility, flexibility, rapid response and multinational cooperation.

Fourth, CJTF was consistent with the drive for cost-effectiveness in defence planning. NATO's goal to be both a crisis manager and a defensive alliance would have to be squared with the financial constraints being experienced in national ministries of defence, particularly for those EU governments keenest to meet the convergence criteria for economic and monetary union. As a result of reduced defence expenditure and force cutbacks across the Alliance in recent years, national capabilities have diminished and the need for precisely applied, multiple-roled, multinational cooperation has therefore increased. During the Cold War, NATO strategy hinged upon vast, peacetime military forces maintained at a reasonably high state of readiness. But large standing forces, with their enormous manpower- and training-related financial burdens, are now an unattainable luxury.

The fifth observation is that, via the NATO–WEU diplomatic relationship, CJTF is the practical means by which the ESDI within NATO will be given military expression. In other words CJTF, as a US-originated and NATO-sponsored idea, will enable the development and growth of ESDI to be carefully controlled; just as there will be no Article 5/non-Article 5 division of labour, neither will the Alliance have separate 'Atlanticist' and 'Europeanist' functions.

Finally, as part of the overall military restructuring of NATO, CJTF could contribute to NATO's relations with the PfP states and ease the enlargement process. According to analysts at the RAND Corporation, the extension of NATO's 'forward presence' on to the territory of new members would be both costly and likely to damage relations with Russia. But NATO's new, multi-functional force posture could provide the way out of the dilemma: 'The projection capabilities that NATO should acquire, in order to carry out enlargement, are precisely the capabilities that will also be required for non-Article 5 missions elsewhere.'[34] And during the anxious weeks before the Madrid Summit, when Polish, Hungarian and Czech hopes for NATO membership seemed to hang in the balance, the establishment of CJTF headquarters seemed to Poland's deputy defence minister to be a good way to cement ties without alarming Russia: 'We do not need heavy deployments of foreign troops. A few hundred soldiers to help run command headquarters would be enough, if only because it is psychologically important.'[35]

Berlin and after

The Berlin communiqué

The Berlin NAC communiqué of 3 June 1996 touched upon all the issues facing NATO: the situation in former Yugoslavia and the conduct of IFOR; the spread of nuclear, biological and chemical weapons of mass destruction; outreach through NACC and PfP, and the enlargement timetable; relations with Russia and Ukraine; the role of the OSCE; the Middle East peace process; and disarmament and arms control.[36] But it was the 'decisive step forward in making the Alliance increasingly flexible and effective to meet new challenges', the apparent 'completion' of the CJTF concept and the stress laid upon 'the development of the [ESDI] within the Alliance' which caused most excitement. At long last, the architectural competition looked to be over, and relieved journalists could report that NATO foreign ministers 'had just agreed to free the European members of NATO from their transatlantic shackles'.[37]

The communiqué endorsed the continuing 'internal adaptation' of NATO and, using by now familiar language, welcomed the CJTF concept as a means to deploy 'more flexible and mobile' forces for 'new missions', 'NATO contingency operations' and 'operations led by the WEU'. Since, in NATO usage, 'contingency operations' can include both Article 5 and non-Article 5 missions, CJTF had by this stage indeed become something of an omnibus concept, capable of meeting traditional and new requirements alike. The most significant part of the document was paragraph 7, which set out the three 'fundamental objectives' underpinning the adaptation process.

The first objective was to maintain the ability to act in collective defence while at the same time developing the means to 'undertake new roles in changing circumstances'. Headquarters and forces would have to be more deployable and mobile, and capable of being sustained in theatre for 'extended periods'. This objective would also involve 'increased participation of [PFP] countries' and the integration of new members into the military structure. But the key point is that one omnibus force structure would meet all tasks and missions. Thus, adaptation would provide the ability 'to mount NATO non-Article 5 operations, guided by the concept of *one system capable of performing multiple functions*'. Similarly, the Alliance would need a '*single* multinational command structure', rather than one for Article 5 and another for non-Article 5 tasks. As a concession to the French and Spanish, the command structure was also to be described as 'renovated'. Once again, the CJTF concept was defined as 'central to our approach for assembling forces for *contingency operations*'(emphases added). And the whole adaptation process would be 'consistent with the goal of building [ESDI] within NATO', enabling 'all European Allies to play a larger role in NATO's military and command structures and, as appropriate, in contingency operations undertaken by the Alliance'. The second objective – the preservation of the transatlantic link – also stressed the need for effective political and military cooperation across the Atlantic, referring to the 'continued involvement of the North American Allies across the command and force structure'.

The third 'fundamental objective' was the development of ESDI within NATO. CJTF would be a vital tool, leading to 'the creation of militarily coherent and effective forces capable of operating under the political control and strategic direction of the WEU'. Forces, assets and headquarters would be identified which could be used for WEU-led operations, subject to various conditions: any forces so identified would be 'separable but not separate', their availability would be 'subject to decision by the NAC', and their use would be monitored and kept under review by the NAC. In conjunction with the development of the CJTF concept, NATO's command structure would be further adapted. Certain NATO personnel would be 'double-hatted' in order to create 'multinational European command arrangements' which were both 'identifiable' as European and firmly part of the NATO structure.

After Berlin: command structure review
The various NAC and DPC/NPG communiqués of June 1996 welcomed the continuing work of the Military Committee's Long Term Study, and looked forward to progress reports in December 1996. But in only a matter of weeks the command structure review was overtaken by disagreements between France and the United States. By summer 1996, the review still had fundamental dilemmas to address and resolve: the number of MSCs within ACE and ACLANT; the number of senior commands to be allocated to European officers (MSC and PSC – both MNCs would continue to be commanded by American officers); whether MSCs should be territorial or functional; where and how to incorporate the CJTF concept into the command structure; and whether the WEU's use of a CJTF would satisfy the demand for an effective and 'visible' ESDI within NATO. These dilemmas came together in August 1996, with the beginnings of what was to be a long-running tug-of-war between Paris and Washington. The French, anxious to see sufficient acknowledgement

of, and reward for, their *rapprochement* with NATO, began to argue for more visibility for the European pillar within NATO's organization and for changes in what might be termed the 'constitution' of the Alliance – the politico-military nexus. The United States' response was shaped by a wish to retain the leadership of the Alliance and – above all else – to ensure that the central principle of unity of command was not undermined. In a letter to his French counterpart in August, President Clinton warned Chirac not to push for too many and extensive changes to NATO's structure. In particular, French calls (backed by Germany) for a European-led AFSOUTH were not acceptable in Washington. AFSOUTH, based in Naples, was commanded by an American officer who also had responsibility for US troops in Bosnia and for the US Sixth Fleet based in the Mediterranean.[38] In a bargaining spirit, the French repeated their plea at the NATO defence ministers' meeting in Bergen, Norway on 26 September 1996. Differences of opinion between Paris and Washington began to deepen, both over AFSOUTH and over French aspirations for a European Deputy SACEUR (able to command WEU-led CJTFs) and – in the much longer term – for a European SACEUR.[39] The clash of wills resulted in a crisp exchange of letters between Clinton and Chirac early in October, in which there seemed to be little ground for compromise over the AFSOUTH issue, and the dispute continued through the autumn and into the new year.

In November 1996 the Alliance's chiefs of defence staff (CHODS), meeting as the Military Committee, produced their final recommendations for revising NATO's command structure.[40] They recommended a reduction in the overall number of NATO headquarters from 65 to about 20. As far as ACLANT was concerned, it was accepted that there should continue to be three MSCs. But on the vexed question of NATO command in Europe, the CHODs could only recommend that the NAC select one of two options, both of which assumed the retention of a fully integrated US–European command structure. The first, and most radical, option was to reduce the MSC level to two functional commands (for convenience and fairness, but for no other territorial rationale), one in the north of Europe and the other in the south, each of which would have all the appearance of a permanent CJTF headquarters.[41] The second option was to retain the existing territorial MSC structure (northwest, centre, south). Most NATO members preferred the first alternative, but the United States (and SHAPE itself) preferred the second, and the debate continued. Within SHAPE, it was argued that only with three MSCs would SACEUR be able to meet his mission to ensure the collective defence capability while being able to mount two non-Article 5 (CJTF) operations simultaneously. Without this capability, it was felt that ESDI within NATO would amount to very little. Furthermore, a three-MSC structure would be one which could accommodate NATO's new members without further restructuring.

In the view of one British commentator – former Chief of the Defence Staff Michael Carver – the MC 'solution' was no such thing. Carver's argument was, essentially, that obsessive attachment to the integrated structure had blinded the review to the logic of post-Cold War European security. A proper debate over territorial versus functional command could not be had if the only outcomes to be contemplated were only those which could fit within and validate the integrated command structure. Carver endorsed a more radical solution – known in NATO jargon as 'binarism', an idea which had earlier been examined and dismissed – by which a straightforward US–European division would be imposed upon the Alliance's command structure, doing away with the shibboleth of integration and the turf battles of recent memory: 'All NATO's integrated commands should be abolished … US forces stationed in Europe or its surrounding waters should be solely under US national command … within the North Atlantic Alliance a European operational and training command should be formed, with subordinate land, air and naval commands, incorporating the forces of those European members of the Alliance who wished to join it.'[42]

NATO's foreign and defence ministers preferred a more measured approach. In their final communiqué of 1996, foreign ministers noted that the two command structure models proposed by the MC would *both* require 'future assessment and subsequent political consideration'. They also rejected any 'binarist' alternative, confirming that the goal of the command structure review remained a 'renovated, single multilateral command structure'.[43] Meeting one week after their foreign ministry colleagues, NATO's defence ministers directed the MC to refine its proposals in time for the regular NAC ministerial meetings in Sintra, Portugal on 29 May 1997. As far as the defence ministers were concerned, the MC should address the following issues in particular:

● the capability and military effectiveness of each of the two command structure alternatives;
● the resource implications of each alternative model;
● the relationship between the various levels of command;
● the type, numbers, locations and responsibilities of sub-regional

level headquarters (i.e. the former MSC and PSC command levels);

● guidelines for the rotation among Alliance members of key command posts.[44]

Work on these and related issues continued into 1997. Tentative agreement on the role and responsibilities of DSACEUR was reached fairly early in the year. The clash between France and the United States, however, continued to overshadow the work of NATO's international and military staffs, with French officials beginning to warn that France – *en pique* – might renege on its *rapprochement*.[45] By early March 1997, it seemed that a compromise might be possible. In line with a German proposal, the United States was reportedly willing to discuss the possibility of surrendering command of AFSOUTH, or sharing the post with a European officer, albeit not for five years.[46] But no sooner was the Franco-US tension beginning to relax than another intra-Alliance disagreement threatened to impede the work being carried out. Turkey, realizing that its membership of the Alliance effectively gave it a veto over the enlargement process, had been probing to see whether the threat of a veto could be used to improve its chances of entry into the EU.[47] Possibly for similar motives, Ankara also began to insist upon being involved in planning any WEU missions which would require the use of NATO assets. Turkey, merely an associate member of WEU by virtue of its membership of NATO, would thereby come closer to the defence and security discussions of the EU/WEU; a prospect which Greece (a full member of the EU, the WEU and NATO) could not contemplate with much composure.

In the event, differences among the allies could not be resolved by July 1997 and the Madrid Summit proved to be something of a damp squib as far as NATO's internal adaptation was concerned. Disagreements developed between Britain and Spain over Gibraltar, between Spain and Portugal over the seas around the Canaries, and between Greece and Turkey over the rights to certain islands in the Aegean.[48] But it was the continued Franco-US dispute which did most to sour the atmosphere at Madrid and prevent final agreement on a new command structure for NATO. The United States remained firmly resistant to French requests for a reorganization (and 'Europeanization') of NATO's command arrangements in the Mediterranean, and dismissed French (and other allies') calls for Romania and Slovenia to be included in the first tranche of enlargement. France, now with a Socialist government containing some 'notable anti-Americans' and others who 'still hanker after a separate European defence organization, outside NATO',[49] remained equally stubborn. Having attached conditions (regarding AFSOUTH and enlargement) to its reintegration into NATO, and having seen those conditions rejected at Madrid, France's only face-saving option was to postpone reintegration indefinitely. President Chirac left Madrid calling for NATO to be made 'lighter, cheaper, more flexible and more effective', and for a 'new balance between Europe and America over the leadership of the alliance'.[50] But just as France had managed to salvage something of its enlargement agenda (by having Romania and Slovenia referred to in glowing terms in the Madrid Declaration), so there was some hope that, after a suitable cooling-off period, the internal adaptation process might be resumed, with the final version of NATO's new command structure document (MC 324) being published in December 1997. The prospect of NATO's DSACEUR (who would also command WEU-led CJTF operations) becoming, in time, a rotational post which France could eventually fill (assuming reintegration into NATO) was thought to be one way to persuade France to soften its stance.[51] And France was also quietly keen to keep the lines of communication open, and to ensure that the internal adaptation process did not stall completely. Not only did France agree at Madrid to continue attending defence ministerial and MC meetings, it also praised the development to date of ESDI within NATO and promised to take part in CJTF operations.[52] Whatever the difficulties over the command structure review, it seemed that the force posture review was looked upon more favourably in Paris.

After Berlin: force posture review
The NAC gave relevant military and political committees until December 1996 to work through the Berlin communiqué – especially paragraph 7, which set out the three fundamental objectives of the adaptation process – before making firm implementation proposals to the NAC. As well as the task of identifying the 'assets' (NATO and national) which might (or might not) be used for WEU-led operations, and reshuffling NATO's command structure to allow CJTF to be deployed painlessly, there were many other matters to be resolved. Further to their May 1996 agreement on exchange of classified documents, liaison arrangements between NATO and the WEU would be examined. NATO political and military staff would help to draw up a planning and training programme for the WEU. And the principle of NAC 'monitoring' and 'review' of WEU use of Alliance assets would have to be clarified. NATO's annual force planning process would also contribute to the adaptation process. The 13

June 1996 DPC/NPG meeting adopted a new set of Force Goals 'as planning targets for our forces and capabilities'.[53] The new Alliance Force Goals would reflect the 'full range of Alliance tasks, including new missions'. Defence ministers placed particular emphasis on having mobile and sustainable forces, able to move within and between theatres and to function effectively once deployed: 'Such capabilities are essential both for the Alliance's collective defence and for the new missions which require the capability for flexible deployments for defence, peacekeeping and crisis management and the capability to counter the risks of the proliferation of weapons of mass destruction (WMD) and their means of delivery.' Once again, the theme of an omnibus force posture loomed large. A considerable amount of work remained to be done before the 'adapted' Alliance could be said to be fully functioning and meeting all its objectives, and much of this effort would be devoted to turning CJTF from a concept – however 'complete' – into a workable mechanism. The DPC/NPG directed that a new set of Force Goals should be drawn up by December, mainly with a view to countering the risks of WMD proliferation.

When NATO defence ministers met at the level of the NAC later in the day on 13 June 1996, they welcomed the approval given to the CJTF earlier in the month by their foreign ministry colleagues. CJTF would provide a link to the WEU and would make it easier for non-NATO countries to join in the Alliance's 'new missions'. But it was especially important that all current allies would be able to participate in the 'CJTF nuclei' established at the various Alliance headquarters. The defence ministers called for the implementation of CJTF to be taken forward 'to the satisfaction of all Allies, as a matter of priority, including in particular the location, size, number and structure of CJTF headquarters elements and their operating procedures', and for a progress report to be made in December 1996. As suggested earlier, the 'location' of CJTF headquarters within the Alliance's command structure was to become particularly divisive during the summer months, not least because the defence ministers had explicitly asked that CJTF implementation should take into account 'the evolving work on the future NATO command structure'.[54]

The next stage in the implementation of the CJTF concept involved revision of the original (1994) idea and the 14 CJTF studies which had been carried out subsequently. The experiences of the NATO-led IFOR in Bosnia received close attention, particularly as regards the integration of non-NATO forces into a multinational operation. Military staff at SHAPE also began to examine the standardization of training and procedures, in order to ensure sufficient interoperability at the outset of any CJTF operation.[55]

The additional, WMD-orientated Force Goals were approved by defence ministers in Brussels in December.[56] The communiqué of the December DPC/NPG meeting refers to work 'now in train to adapt the Alliance's military structures' and explains what much of that work was about. National defence plans for 1997–2001 and beyond had been reviewed, and defence ministers had accepted a 'five-year force plan aimed at the continuing adaptation of our defence plans to match the new security situation'. Modernization of NATO's force posture would continue, although the defence ministers acknowledged that budgetary constraints imposed by some member states could delay the implementation of a new, more lean and effective overall force posture. The force planning process would continue into 1997, paying particular attention to the following areas:

- deployable command, control and communications (C^3) systems;
- strategic mobility (i.e. heavy lift by sea or air);
- sustainability (i.e. logistic support in theatre);
- ground-based air defence;
- strategic surveillance and intelligence systems (i.e. the employment of high-value reconnaissance satellites and aircraft).

A detachable and deployable command and control (C^2) apparatus, along with highly mobile forces and sound intelligence, had all by now become central to the development of the CJTF idea. When, later the same day, the defence ministers reshuffled themselves to become the NAC in defence ministerial session, they recorded the progress which had been made in refining the CJTF concept by the end of the year. The defence ministers 'noted with satisfaction that the implementation of the [CJTF] concept is well under way'. A 'phased implementation' had been agreed which should, in time, enable NATO to deploy 'both small and large-scale land and sea-based CJTF headquarters to conduct the full range of CJTF operations'. CJTF headquarters were being developed 'primarily' for non-Article 5 crisis management operations in which non-NATO nations could also participate. The use of CJTFs for the core, Article 5 task of collective self-defence was, however, not ruled out. With the blessing of the NAC, CJTF headquarters would also be made available for WEU-led operations and would thus 'contribute to the development of ESDI within the Alliance'. Two military staffs had been established to deal with the implementation of CJTF: a Capabilities Co-ordination Cell (CCC) within the IMS at NATO headquarters, to assist the MC with CJTF related matters, and a Combined Joint Planning Staff (CJPS) at SHAPE headquarters to provide both MNCs with a central planning staff for CJTF operations. Three MSC headquarters – Striking Fleet Atlantic, AFCENT and AFSOUTH – had been chosen to be the first 'parent headquarters for CJTF nuclei'. Deployment trials would begin 'as soon as practicable'. Consistent with earlier pronouncements, the trials would focus initially on NATO operations, dealing with the WEU-led variant at a later date.[57] By the end of 1996 the implementation of the CJTF concept was, plainly, absorbing a great deal of energy, imagination and planning time.

By mid-1997 the CJTF concept had developed considerably and become an elaborate blueprint for NATO operations. A politico-military framework had been agreed, around which NATO's military leaders could develop CJTF doctrine, standard operating procedures and training objectives. Early in 1997 the Military Committee issued its directive for the implementation of the CJTF concept (MC 389). This paper became the catalyst for a series of command post exercises, computer-assisted exercises and live exercises during 1997 and 1998, and for the develop-ment of formal, agreed CJTF HQ doctrine. The aim of the exercise programme was to test a number of aspects of the CJTF concept, including the notion that an embryonic (or 'nucleus') CJTF HQ could be earmarked at a 'parent' headquarters (MSC or lower), the ease with which a full-establishment CJTF headquarters could be detached from its host and deployed into the field, and the way in which the CJTF HQ would cooperate with component (i.e. single-service) commands further down the NATO chain.

Yet, by mid-1977, several important issues remained to be resolved. One problem was the complement of a full-establishment CJTF HQ: the fact that a headquarters might absorb over 450 staff officers and soldiers before a single infantryman could be deployed would not sit easily with a declining NATO manpower base and would be unpopular with those concerned with disproportionate 'teeth-to-tail' ratios. The overall cost of the CJTF programme became another serious issue. It was not at all clear that NATO's budget could fund both the enlargement programme and the development of the CJTF, even after closing the account for Article 5 collective defence training. Then there was the question of sustaining CJTF operations. MC 389 contemplated a 'small option' CJTF of two or three thousand troops, and a 'large option' involving thirty or forty thousand, with both being in place for up to two years. But, as Britain's experience in Northern Ireland has demonstrated over many years, even the 'small option' would create considerable demands if the troops in theatre were to be efficient, effective and happy. Other, more practical problems included the compatibility and standardization of communications equipment by all those taking part in a CJTF (NATO and non-NATO);[58] the harmonization of rules of engagement for CJTF participants; and procedures for the combined targeting of air power. With detailed staff work and an exercise programme to test ideas, none of these problems could be considered insurmountable. However, the force posture review was effectively brought to a halt by disagreements over NATO's new command structure. Until consensus could be reached on the broad character of NATO's command structure (i.e. the number of levels of command), on the number and character of headquarters at each level, and on the relationship between joint and component command structures, the CJTF concept would be unable to leave the nest.

After Berlin: strategy review
At the start of this chapter the Rome Strategic Concept was described as 'a relatively stable feature of the NATO adaptation process'; nevertheless, since Madrid the Alliance's strategy has been brought back into the limelight, in order to ensure that it remains 'fully consistent with Europe's new security situation and challenges'.[59] Understandably, institutions are generally reluctant to rewrite documents which could be said to be of fundamental – even 'constitutional' – significance; the Rome Strategic Concept is one such document. Yet there is, at the very least, a case for refreshing the language of the Concept. With several references to the 'USSR' and the 'Soviet Union', the document could be said to be too evocative of the Cold War. Other criticisms are more fundamental. One misgiving, often voiced by US analysts, is that the European members of the Alliance are still 'psychologically wedded to the concept of security as territorial defence'.[60] Continued attachment to the territorial defence of Europe, it is argued, is inappropriate, given the absence of a major threat. And, in any case, to see security in terms only of territory is to fail to understand international security after the Cold War; how can environmental or water security be understood by a mind-set rooted in the GDP and the battle for the European Central Front?

Another objection to the status quo is that NATO's command structure and force posture reviews have taken it in the direction of ad hoc 'coalitions of the able and willing', while the Alliance's core strategy remains stuck in the rigid 'all for one and one for all' commitment made in Article 5 of the North Atlantic Treaty. It could also be argued that in the process of adapting itself NATO has become distracted by too many other, non-military issues. Driven by the need to forge links with other European institutions, to satisfy the demands and *amour propre* of individual members, and to take on new members, NATO may have allowed its political dimension to outweigh and obscure its core military function.

A strategy review could be a good opportunity to address these complaints. Modifying the language of the Concept should be a relatively straightforward task, and might be a useful step in cementing the new relationship between NATO and Russia. A review might demonstrate to the European allies the perils of introspection and isolationism, and emphasize the need for a broad-minded approach to European and world security. A strategic stocktaking might enable the gap to be closed between current and anticipated Alliance practice and the strategic tradition embodied in Article 5, and might also remove any ambiguity and controversy within and surrounding the Alliance.

On the other hand, it could be that a review of the Concept will produce little more than is already known, and may even be counter-productive. Strategy is all about defining a relationship between the political and military arenas. But the continuing processes of outreach and enlargement, and the arrival of the term 'self-differentiation' in the Alliance's vocabulary,[61] suggest that one half of the strategic relation-ship, the political element, will remain, intentionally, changeable and unpredictable. What is more, with its emphasis on capability-based, rather than threat-based military planning, it is clear that the Alliance is proposing to respond to emergencies and crises on more of an ad hoc basis: in other words, the military half of the strategic relationship is also to be allowed to float more freely. Given the uncertainties of European and international security, all this flexibility is no doubt a good thing. But it is difficult to see how it could be translated into some sort of strategic vision. NATO's military missions, and participation in them, might have to be organized on a more ad hoc basis, but can strategy itself be ad hoc? NATO's '*Very* New Strategic Concept' could amount to planning for military operations at unpredictable levels in unpredictable places against unpredictable enemies to achieve unpredictable goals on behalf of an unpredictable collection of allies (and perhaps a few non-allies, too).

It might be argued that the review should try to nudge NATO strategy away from these shifting sands towards the firmer ground of Article 5.

With collective defence as its unequivocal strategic core, there ought to be no need to worry about how, or whether, the Alliance's ad hoc, non-Article 5 tasks could be translated into a strategic formula. But collective defence is not fashionable at the moment; it is too heavy-handed for the tasks NATO expects to carry out, is too costly to be prepared for properly, and may be seen as confrontational by Russia. Collective defence is not the answer, and it is not on Article 5 that the Alliance's future success will depend. That said, it is not easy to conceive of a military alliance of sovereign states being, at bottom, anything other than collective and territorial. Residual and symbolic it may be, but if the 'Three Musketeers' collective defence commitment were to be removed, the Alliance could collapse politically and militarily.

With an 'ad hoc strategy' difficult to imagine, and with NATO's traditional strategy too rigid and inappropriate, an alternative is needed. Given the idea of 'self-differentiation', and the thrust of the Alliance's internal adaptation, the alternative might be to accept that NATO has already come as close as it can – or needs – to a strategy 'fully consistent with Europe's new security situation and challenges'.

The CJTF concept is key to understanding the character and potential of the new NATO. Development of the concept is expected to be completed during 1997 and 1998. CJTF has been hailed as innovative and dynamic, and expectations of it have been mounting. The significance of CJTF is that it has become much more than just a tool for multi-national, joint service military planning. CJTF is common to many aspects of NATO's internal adaptation and straddles the divide between politics and the military. The concept not only features prominently in the reviews of the Alliance's command structure and force posture, it also serves the political function of enabling NATO to breathe life into the ESDI (via WEU-led CJTF operations), and should enable NATO to cooperate with the armed forces of new and candidate members without confronting Russia.

Barring the unlikely emergence of a threat of Cold War proportions, NATO's strategy may already be as effective as could be expected. With CJTF, NATO has found a means with which to satisfy urgent political demands (institutional and national), to bridge the gap between the Alliance's political and military functions, and to enable military planning across the spectrum of operations from crisis management to collective defence. It would not be too much of an exaggeration, therefore, to say that NATO's strategy, its command structure and its force posture have all become one, in the form of the CJTF. If the object of NATO strategy is to forge a dynamic politico-military relationship among the allies, it must also be defensive, and must resist attempts to divide allies or break the connection between the political and military elements. The problem is that the developing Alliance could be all too vulnerable to just such an assault. As NATO becomes increasingly an 'alliance of choice' rather than an 'alliance of necessity', the will to cooperate politically and militarily can no longer be taken for granted. Support for NATO will increasingly be contingent upon its operational effectiveness and relevance. The priority must therefore be to make the new, adapted NATO work. To continue the search for a perfect, strategic Holy Grail might be to divert energy from this urgent task. Worse still, to open a full strategic review at this stage in its development might show to the world that, for all its excellent organization and military potential, at its heart NATO has become too much of a 'virtual alliance', with several chinks in its politico-military armour.

Conclusion CJTF

Work will continue on the adaptation of NATO's military structure, at least until December 1997. The overall aim of the exercise has been to enable the Alliance to respond effectively to all possible or likely missions, with the involvement of new members and non-members, and to breathe life into the ESDI. In time, the outcome of the process should be a triad incorporating a remodelled command structure, a new, leaner and more mobile force posture, and a revised (or, perhaps, reaffirmed) strategy. Each element of the triad has CJTF at its centre. In operational terms, the CJTF concept is nothing new or spectacular. But at the same time it is much more than a politico-military leasing arrangement by which Europeans will be able to borrow NATO equipment when needed. The CJTF idea is novel in two ways. First, it is a common, 'omnibus' answer to many problems and tensions within the post-Cold War Alliance. Second, it is an attempt to institutionalize ad hoc, spontaneous military cooperation in crisis management and defence. This latter feature is consistent with the 'capability-based' or 'task-based' approach to defence thinking, and the 'virtual alliance', outlined in chapter 2, and it may suffer similar credibility problems. CJTF may prove to be incoherent, unwieldy or unable to serve so many masters. Or Alliance members may prove unwilling to underwrite the political, military and financial costs of the enterprise. But if CJTF withers on the vine, then recent progress towards a Euro-Atlantic defence and security framework for the twenty-first century could be blocked. Without the will to make the admittedly complex CJTF scheme work, and in the absence of a convincing, unifying, threat-based rationale for military cooperation, the Alliance may discover to its cost that it has spent much of the past seven years attempting to substitute process for substance.

Chapter 5

Testing the consensus

Introduction

The Berlin communiqué of 3 June 1996 referred to the three 'fundamental objectives' which would guide NATO's efforts to adapt itself to post-Cold War circumstances. The first objective was to 'ensure the Alliance's military effectiveness', the second was to 'preserve the transatlantic link', and the third was to develop the 'European Security and Defence Identity within the Alliance'.[1] These goals soon became something of a collective mantra, repeated quietly but determinedly by all those officials and politicians who subscribed to the arrangements put in place at Berlin.[2] Pursuit of the first of these objectives – military effectiveness – has been addressed in chapter 4. The second and third objectives – preserving the transatlantic link and developing ESDI within NATO – are the focus of the present chapter, which is therefore concerned less with the form and function of the Alliance than with its political underpinning.

The 'new' or 'relaunched' NATO depends for its success upon the achievement of all three objectives. This is not, however, a new challenge, one peculiar to post-Cold War Alliance politics. Military effectiveness – the first objective – has been revisited periodically in NATO's history, usually prompting a change of strategy and doctrine. The second and third objectives have been, similarly, leitmotifs in the Alliance's history. But neither of these objectives has ever been achieved completely and conclusively, nor has a way been found to ensure that efforts to achieve one would not have a distorting effect on the other. It has been more common for the Alliance to muddle through, relying upon a fairly steady transatlantic consensus to withstand periods of crisis and transformation. Chapter 3 has shown how this consensus began to operate most recently, with the four major powers slowly converging on a point where the ideas described in chapter 4 could begin to put down roots.

Perversely, the task of this chapter is to seek out chinks in the armour, to search for factors which might undermine the transatlantic consensus and prevent the necessary further evolution of the Alliance. One such factor is NATO enlargement which, although now under way with the agreement of all NATO members, has led to heated debate on both sides of the Atlantic. A great deal of uncertainty remains over the wisdom of the enlargement project, and although critics of enlargement may, for the time being, have been silenced, they will no doubt resume their campaign when the national ratification processes begin.[3]

The Franco-US dispute suggests there may be other, more basic, flaws in the diplomatic concoction served up at Berlin and elaborated over the following 15 months. Several awkward questions lie just below the surface of the debate. Why does the United States wish to remain involved in European defence and security? Does the United States wish to dominate, lead or act jointly with its allies? To what extent does the military adaptation described earlier satisfy US requirements? And as for the Europeans, do they want the United States to remain? Do they want to be led by the Americans? Do they still hanker after their own defence and security outside the umbrella provided by the United States and NATO, and if so how capable are they of expressing themselves militarily? And how well – and genuinely – do the evolving command structure and force posture allow for the expression of 'ESDI within NATO'? France had wanted the Berlin communiqué to describe ESDI as a 'permanent and visible' part of NATO, but even this relatively undemonstrative form of words was too much for other delegations to accept.[4] Could it therefore be said that 'visibility' – or lack of it – is all that is now left of the 'Europeanist' approach to the defence and security of western Europe? Have Europeanist expectations been reduced to hollow rhetoric?

The chapter is divided into three parts. The first part begins by asking what US government officials and media understood to have been achieved in Berlin in June 1996, and then examines US critiques of the US–European defence and security partnership after the Cold War. Similarly, the second part begins by recording first impressions among the leading European participants at Berlin, but then focuses on aspirations for a more discretely European security and defence identity. How potent are these aspirations, and are they likely to be satisfied by the formula agreed at Berlin? The third part examines the defence industry and asks whether present trends point towards cooperation or competition across the Atlantic.

US perspectives

Impressions of the Berlin agreement
Shortly before NATO foreign ministers assembled in Berlin, the US approach to the ministerial was summarized in a background briefing in Washington by an (unnamed) official of the US State Department.[5] The briefing set out by now familiar themes. NATO's internal adaptation would serve several purposes; NATO was confronted by new tasks after the Cold War and was on the verge of accepting new members. NATO was also adapting in order to 'define a new type of relationship across the Atlantic and to make NATO a common enterprise. The important thing here is that this is not Europe developing separate facilities; this is using NATO for common goals.' In order to cement this new relationship, NATO would have to become a 'dual-purpose tool for both a broad Atlantic security relationship and as the embodiment of the [ESDI]'. The European allies would be given 'visibility' and 'capability' within the Alliance, enabling them to carry out operations through the WEU. Accommodating France within NATO was, evidently, an important aspect of – and rationale for – the State Department's approach to NATO adaptation. *As a consequence of* the proposed changes, France would move towards the integrated structure, with more substantial results possible in the longer term; 'the logic of this, if the project works, is that France will rejoin the integrated military structure.' But amid the great expectations, there was also a sense of caution. When it came to the question of the United States providing material support to a WEU-led operation, the expressions 'if appropriate' and 'maybe' crept into the official's language. These two themes – accommodating the French while being cautious about the US commitment – dominated the US position in the ensuing weeks.

During and after the ministerial, senior US officials were gushing in their praise for France's *rapprochement* with NATO. In his address to the NAC, US Secretary of State Warren Christopher took a slightly different approach from that taken by his junior official in Washington a few days earlier, being less willing to see the work of the ministerial as a sweetener for French re-entry into NATO. Christopher applauded France's 'historic step in drawing closer to the military side of NATO', and Chirac's 'historic choice to pursue ESDI within the Alliance', a decision which 'in a very real sense' made progress at the ministerial possible.[6] The same chain of reasoning was used later the following month by Robert Hunter, the US Ambassador to NATO. Like Christopher, Hunter applauded France's 'far-reaching' and 'politically courageous' decisions. Hunter saw the French moves as *enabling* NATO adaptation, and did not argue that the purpose of the adaptation was to please the French.[7] Nevertheless, 'pleasing the French' was clearly on the minds of some US officials during and after the Berlin ministerial. At a press briefing immediately after the meeting, one 'senior defense official' (unnamed) from the Pentagon reflected that 'one of the important things this [the outcome of the ministerial] does is it brings the French closer to the alliance. They fully participated in all the decisions.'[8] Other media and official comment indicated or implied that the adaptation exercise was indeed being shaped by the perceived need to accede to some French wishes, partly to ease France's return to NATO, partly to create a military structure more conducive to cooperation with NATO's partners in the PfP programme, and partly in order that France would not obstruct the admission of new members in 1997.[9]

It would almost certainly be an exaggeration to suggest that their rank alone led senior and more junior US officials to different conclusions regarding the approach to France and the broad nature and significance of the Berlin agreement. But the political level to which these officials reported may have affected the manner in which they explained the outcome of the meeting. The State Department evidently approached the Berlin ministerial with a degree of caution regarding the depth of US commitment to any new arrangement. The explanation for this is simple: whatever the outcome, it would have to be 'sold' to a wary US public and an even more sceptical US Congress. It is clear from press briefings and speeches that Christopher, Hunter and other senior officials were having to 'think upwards', to evaluate the Berlin ministerial in ways which would elicit the best response in the United States. Alexander Vershbow, senior director for European affairs at the National Security Council, and special assistant to President Clinton, saw the trade-off in clear enough terms. If the European allies could 'prove themselves capable in practice of shouldering greater responsibility for European security within NATO', then it would make it easier in the long-term 'to maintain US domestic support for the alliance'.[10] Another 'senior American official' commented: 'We've wanted for years to see the Europeans shoulder a bigger burden inside the alliance, and Congress would like to see that, too.'[11] And Robert Hunter, in his speech to a WEU-sponsored conference in Washington late in July 1996, went so far as to state that 'the single greatest task I have is bringing to the United States, and particularly to the US Congress, knowledge of what is being done at NATO and WEU, and to underscore what it is that our European friends and allies are doing to demonstrate their own added responsibility for trans-Atlantic security.'[12]

In order to shape the Berlin ministerial for domestic US consumption, it was important, conversely, not to be too fulsome. If the result were described as a wholly new arrangement, this would be too much of a break with the past and might invite the criticism that the United States had embarked on a new, multilateral military alliance without due consultation and ratification by Congress. As a result, there was a thick vein of conservatism in official pronouncements regarding the purposes and structure of the 'new' NATO. Warren Christopher took pains to point out that NATO had, all along, been intended to be a 'permanent alliance', that NATO remained the 'linchpin' of the US engagement in Europe, and that 'the qualities that have made NATO the most successful alliance in history – its core purpose of collective defense, its integrated command structure, and the transatlantic link – must and will be preserved.'[13] There was 'no substitute for NATO', and Christopher argued that the Berlin ministerial would preserve, rather than supplant, the tried and trusted alliance.[14]

For the same reasons, it was essential to avoid any suggestion that the Europeans could now be capable of acting without US help or leadership. This concern manifested itself in two ways. In the first place, it had to be shown that the Europeans were not simply being given a ready-made package of forces and arrangements with which they could do as they wished, but that they would have to 'seize this opportunity and build upon it', developing the WEU and creating an ESDI within the framework approved by NATO and the US.[15] Second, while 'eager to suggest to a wary Congress that Europe will shoulder more of the transatlantic defense burden', US officials tried to 'play down the practical consequences' of the ministerial by admitting that they could barely conceive of any security crises which would not involve NATO and the United States: 'In the real world, when real threats develop, the United States will be there.'[16] In a press conference before the NAC defence ministerial session on 13 June 1996, Hunter underlined this position: 'We, the United States, expect to be involved in I would say virtually any security concern here in Europe, and certainly anything of any major significance.'[17] And in the US official view, the Berlin ministerial contained several commitments which were consistent with the principle that the US and NATO should remain at the centre of all things concerned with European security:

- US leadership of the Alliance would remain unchallenged;
- NATO's unified command structure would remain intact;[18]
- NATO would tackle both Article 5 and non-Article 5 missions;
- ESDI would be constructed within NATO, rather than as an alternative to it;
- WEU-led operations would require the unanimous approval of the NAC;[19]
- forces and command systems earmarked for possible WEU-led operations were to be considered 'separable but not separate' from the overall NATO structure;
- NATO's institutional partner would be the relatively unknown WEU, rather than the EU – which was perceived to be flawed by the 'failure' of Bosnia, more strident and ambitious, and altogether less biddable.[20]

US impressions of the Berlin ministerial were shaped by two considerations, therefore. The European endeavour was to be accommodated and encouraged, in order to develop an alliance more appropriate for the post-Cold War world and in order that the transatlantic defence and security burden should be shared more equitably. On the other hand, the outcome of the ministerial was to be carefully constrained, in order that the glue which bound NATO together and which kept the US involved – in a leadership capacity – in European defence and security should not be weakened. All this led the United States into a mildly self-contradictory position regarding Berlin. Meeting the press after the ministerial, Warren Christopher was challenged by one journalist to comment on the perceived gulf between 'substance' and 'ritual' in the discussions. The journalist noted that US officials spoke of attempts to give the European Union [*sic*] 'a developing sense of security identity within NATO', while being unable to 'think of a way in which this might be used'. Furthermore, given the NAC unanimity proviso, US officials were also hard pressed to 'think of a way in which the United States would ever allow something to happen that it didn't want to happen'. Christopher's response to this well-targeted challenge was muddled,[21] lending weight to one analyst's dismissal of the 'Europeanization' of NATO as a 'convenient myth'.[22]

A new deal in transatlantic security
The burden-sharing debate has been a hardy perennial in NATO's history. During the Cold War, the debate was largely a matter of the United States cajoling west Europeans into paying a larger proportion of the bill for their own defence and security in Europe. But since the United States was anxious to remain the unrivalled leader of the Western Alliance, it was important that, whatever the Europeans could do, they should remain individually and corporately subordinate. For Washington, this meant a policy of 'divide and conquer through bilateral diplomacy' so that any attempt to construct a rival security and defence organization in and for Europe would be nipped in the bud.[23] For Europe, and for NATO as a whole, the result was often confusion. It was generally understood that if the Europeans were neither able to organize themselves into a more efficient wing of the Alliance, nor willing to commit more resources to the common cause, then the very idea of a security partnership could be at stake. If, however, the Europeans could at least organize themselves better, while remaining reluctant or unable to contribute more, US critics (particularly in Congress) might see a caucus of free-riders intent on unbalancing the partnership and undermining US leadership. But if the European allies could make both an efficient and a well-funded contribution to their own defence, what need would there be for US assistance and leadership, and indeed for NATO?

Judging by comments made during and shortly after the Berlin ministerial, Cold War-style thinking has a long shelf-life. US officials appeared to agree that US leadership and domination of any reformed transatlantic defence and security partnership, along with guaranteeing the primacy of NATO over any European rival, were essential policy goals. Officials were also conscious of the need to 'sell the deal' to the US public and Congress. But while they may have been concerned to explain *how* the United States should be involved in European defence and security after the Cold War, the question *why* the United States should be so engaged tended to be answered somewhat less fully. There is an occasional tendency among US officials to dump the pragmatic diplomat's calculus of national self-interest and security and resort to idealism, romanticism, history and hyperbole when describing the foundations of the US–European relationship. NATO has been described by one US official as 'really nothing more than an organizational embodiment of a community which is nearly three hundred years old'.[24] Such sentimental generalizations also crept into some of the speeches referred to earlier: the US had a 'very fundamental interest' in a 'strong trans-Atlantic alliance'; US security was 'bound up' with Europe just as European security was 'bound up' with the United States; and, after the Cold War, US 'security interests' in Europe were 'too fundamental for us to disengage'.[25] Plenty of resounding rhetoric, but based more on assumption than analysis; what were these 'security interests', why were they so 'fundamental', and how and why were they shared with Europe?

There are three possible explanations for this apparent reluctance to venture beyond oratory when discussing the essence of the US–European relationship. One explanation might be that rhetoric is used to obfuscate the issues and divert debate. The US foreign and defence policy-making elite may regard the US–European relationship as essential. But because this relationship is in reality so fragile, and because the US public and Congress are so sceptical, officials resort to the simple debating device of presenting the relationship as an unquestionable, objective necessity. Frank and open debate would invite, and dignify, powerful and popular criticism in the United States and is therefore avoided. An alternative explanation is that, far from being a façade erected by cynical manipulators of public opinion, a dynamic, transatlantic 'community' of nations, cultures, values and so forth does indeed exist, but is so abstract, and difficult to describe, that busy officials find it better assumed than analysed.

The third explanation is that US officials are lazy salesmen who have not conducted much market research among those – the US public and Congress – to whom they must 'sell' their vision of the post-Cold War transatlantic relationship. Isolationists, unilateralists and protectionists all have a voice in the US foreign policy debate, albeit at the periphery. But if US officials believe that their only task is to see off these marginal, extremist views with appeals to undefined 'fundamental interests' and the like, then they overlook the widespread public (and Congressional) misgivings upon which the extremists draw, and are tilting at windmills. Good market research would show that US public opinion – although only rarely engaged in foreign policy issues and relations with Europe – is not in fact isolationist, but is certainly much less tolerant than before of any free-riding by allies of the United States.

Constructively minded critics of the US security relationship with Europe argue that burden-sharing discussions in the narrow Cold War tradition are no longer relevant. Instead, what is required is, first, a thorough reassessment of the mutual interests upon which the relation-ship is based, followed by a genuine and equitable allocation of risks and costs. To argue, as did Anthony Lake (Assistant to President Clinton for National Security Affairs) in October 1996, that 'in this new world of possibility – but also of risk – the need for America's global leadership is undiminished,'[26] rather misses the point. It is not US 'leadership' that is needed, but 'partnership' between equals who must share not only costs but responsibilities. The risks and responsibilities of the post-Cold War world – the proliferation of WMD, the protection of Persian Gulf oil reserves, the calls for peacekeeping and peace enforcement – affect Europeans as much as they affect Americans, and must take any partnership between the two beyond the narrow confines of NATO's Eurocentric strategy and force posture of the Cold War.

The United States *needs partners*, not only because even superpowers hate to feel lonely, but also because, militarily, the United States cannot do everything and welcomes the self-generated authority and legitimacy of a multilateral operation. But the United States also *expects partnership*, in a relationship which is more open-ended, outward-looking, adaptable, proactive and equitable. David Gompert of the RAND Corporation has argued that the United States, far from being isolationist and protectionist, is fully committed to participating in the global economy and to ensuring the survival of that economic system.[27] But the United States cannot participate and compete on equal terms if its strategic partners (and main economic competitors) expect it to carry a disproportionate global security burden. With the passing of the Cold War antagonism, it is becoming uncomfortably apparent in the United States that America's allies are willing to see their strategic leader of Cold War days become the economic follower of the new millennium. It is as if the United States is no longer expected merely to tolerate free-riders, but must now pay extra for them to move ahead on a faster bus.

Burden-sharing remains a live issue in the United States. But, at least in the public domain, the terms of debate have moved along and no longer revolve around whether – or how much – the Europeans should contribute to their own, local security. Calls for a 'new compact' or an 'ambitious partnership' between the United States and its European allies,[28] and even for a comprehensive 'New Transatlantic Security Bargain' leading to a 'fundamental redefinition of transatlantic burden sharing',[29] amount to a demand that the Europeans should not just do more, but do it differently. In an ironic reversal of the popular criticism of US foreign policy during the first half of the twentieth century, Europeans are now called upon to shed *their* insularity, isolationism and 'strategic myopia'.[30] Europeans are urged to eschew the outmoded concept of territorial defence to which they are 'psychologically wedded' and develop forces and strategies more appropriate for 'projecting power outward'.[31]

US perspectives on the Berlin ministerial and its implications were therefore an uneasy amalgam of Cold War-style thinking – where the security of the European region, US leadership of NATO and burden-sharing continue to be at the centre of discussions – with a more populist approach which stressed the sharing of responsibilities as well as burdens, in a partnership which is global rather than European. These perspectives offer very different 'futures' for the US–European security relationship, but both require the European allies to do more. This is the crux of the matter. Whether NATO's mission after the Cold War should be conservative and Eurocentric, or more expansive in structure and outlook, there is broad agreement that the European allies must be seen to be contributing more, and differently. There is more interest in results than in structures; the European allies are at times perceived to be unhealthily institution- rather than goal-oriented. But structures are, of course, also important; if a more progressive, dynamic transatlantic relationship is to develop, one which both requires and enables the European allies to make a larger and more authoritative contribution to the common weal, then the institution which lies at the centre of the relationship – NATO – must also change.

Various models for a 'new' NATO feature in the US foreign and defence policy debate. The European allies might be invited to take on the responsibility for their own regional defence and security, freeing the United States to deal with insecurity elsewhere (in the Persian Gulf, for example). This model, however, seems more likely to unravel than to cement a US–European partnership. More sophisticated suggestions accept that for NATO to remain unified and dynamic, all allies must be involved in all contingencies (or at least have that opportunity). Precisely how to coordinate US and European contributions is a more open question. As a powerful symbol of its continuing commitment to Europe, the United States might lead in matters of European security, with the bulk of NATO's 'European' force posture being American. The European allies would contribute to the force posture but would be concerned primarily with leading in, and providing for, non-European contingencies, to which the United States would also contribute. A more likely scenario would see European allies lead in matters of European security, with significant US military assistance, while making their own contribution to US leadership in extra-European operations. Implicit in all this, of course, is the assumption that the United States is ready to work with its European allies in this way; the degree to which European contributions should be written into US strategic planning became a prominent feature of the debate surrounding the 1996–7 US Quadrennial Defense Review.

Common to these and other structural models are a number of expectations. The first is that the 'new' transatlantic security relationship must have at least two areas of interest – perhaps Europe and the 'rest of the world' – and be equally ready to deal with crises in and beyond Europe. The second expectation is that NATO should adapt its strategic concept to enable defence and security to be treated in other than strictly territorial terms. This may entail a return to the pre-Korean War days of Regional Planning Groups, and perhaps even a rewording of Article 5 of the Washington Treaty. Finally, the 'new' NATO must have two politico-military pillars – North American and European, equally well-built and well-finished – rather than one large and unwieldy pillar enjoying the doubtful support of a badly built flying buttress. It is to the design, structure and reliability of a putative European pillar that this chapter now turns.

European perspectives

Impressions of the Berlin agreement

The responses of the three main European allies to the Berlin ministerial ranged from the conservative Atlanticism of London, through Bonn's anxiety to show that the agreement held something for everyone, to a lingering radical Europeanism in Paris. In spite of the generally warm welcome for the Berlin communiqué, significant differences of opinion remained – particularly between the French and British. More important, the emerging transatlantic consensus, on the value of the communiqué and the purpose of NATO's internal adaptation, was not as watertight as might have been supposed.

Britain was reported as having gone along 'quite happily' with the ministerial, although there had, clearly, been moments of friction when British officials felt compelled to defend the importance of NATO and the US connection. According to Foreign Secretary Malcolm Rifkind, 'There was a suggestion at one stage that there should be a separate European command structure … It did not survive, nor did it deserve to … NATO continues to be the only credible force when it comes to combat operations or operations of any scale.' Similarly, Michael Portillo, British Defence Secretary, dismissed the suggestion that the goal of the adaptation was to provide the EU with a discrete military identity. Portillo reportedly 'insisted that neither NATO nor the WEU could submit itself to policies made by the EU'; 'The WEU is not, and will not be, a European substitute for NATO.'[32] Addressing the WEU Assembly in Paris immediately after the Berlin ministerial, Rifkind argued that the challenge had been to find, in one strategic concept, a way to bring Atlanticism and Europeanism together. NATO's internal adaptation had met the challenge: 'We can now develop a European defence identity without weakening NATO.'[33] The British media were equally cautious in their interpretation of the communiqué: the Europeans had by no means been given a free hand to use NATO strategic assets since much of this equipment was US-owned, and 'what the US gives, it can take away'; the new arrangement was, in part, merely an expedient to enable agreement between the French and Americans over the enlargement issue; and the agreement contained 'many potential pitfalls'.[34]

Some officials were prepared to be rather more bullish about NATO's prospects after the Berlin ministerial. In a speech in London early in October 1996, Britain's Ambassador to NATO was impressed by the high morale now pervading the Alliance: 'NATO feels like an organization with a role and a future.'[35] Part of NATO's success he attributed to the internal reforms – an unglamorous, but 'radical' part (and 'one of the most important') of NATO's post-Cold War agenda. The significance of the internal adaptation process lay in what the ambassador saw as 'the best news on the defence front in the last decade – the chance to reconcile a genuine European defence capability with a reformed and still central NATO. The secret lies in building the [ESDI] within NATO, using NATO assets and skills for WEU operations, rather than trying forlornly to build it elsewhere.' The WEU lay at the centre of the new ESDI within NATO formula, in an arrangement which would not work if the EU IGC decided in 1997 to 'subordinate' the WEU to the EU. This predictable, British view would have elicited an equally predictable response from those European allies who saw some form of merger between the two institutions as a real prospect. But with one other comment, concerning the broader debate about the very substance of 'ESDI within NATO', the ambassador was too quick to claim victory. One of the 'key ingredients' in the 'culture change' within the Alliance was France's 'readiness to see the [ESDI] embedded in NATO'. Before too long, however, it would become clear that, as far as Paris was concerned, 'embedded' did not mean 'held captive'.

For all his enthusiasm for a Europeanist future in defence and security, Germany's foreign minister, Klaus Kinkel, appeared to see the communiqué as a triumph for common sense, and was careful to avoid institutional or geographical specifics: 'In the long run, it is neither in the American nor the European interest that we have to call our American friends each time something flares up somewhere.'[36] Indeed, judging by the comments of Volker Rühe, Germany's defence minister, speaking in November 1996, Bonn's policy was to sound as positive as possible on the subject of NATO internal adaptation, without venturing into too much – potentially controversial – detail.[37] Thus, the new NATO would 'reflect a new balance of burden and responsibility sharing between Europe and North America', and there would be 'drastic horizontal and vertical rationalization'. Rühe applauded the results of the Alliance's internal adaptation for the safest, least controversial reason of all – that it would avoid the duplication of structures and the waste of money and resources. Perhaps rather prematurely, Rühe considered that the Americans and Europeans had 'finally understood each other's perceptions and agreed on the principal consequences'; the United States remained 'committed to stability in and for Europe', and the Europeans, for their part, were 'ready to take on a bigger share of the burdens and responsibilities'. In Rühe's view, Atlanticism provided the best way forward: 'Euro-purists are always tempted to centre their thinking on Europe only, thereby neglecting the fact that European security has an Atlantic dimension, and that Europe's ability to act can only be constituted within the framework of NATO.'

For Bonn, the attraction of the Berlin communiqué was that it represented a workable compromise between different approaches to European security, but did not require longer-term, more visionary objectives to be jettisoned. A reminder that these goals would still be pursued was provided by Germany's Ambassador to NATO, in a speech to the Royal United Services Institute on 22 November 1996. Von Richthofen argued that the process of integration in the EU would be 'enhanced by strengthening the Union's capacity to act in the field of common foreign and security policy'. This strengthening might include the introduction of a CFSP planning unit, a 'Secretary General for CFSP', the formal incorporation of the Petersberg tasks into the amended EU treaty, the introduction of qualified majority voting, and a role for the European Council in providing 'guidelines in matters of defence policy through the WEU'.[38]

Many of these objectives, however distant, would have been beyond serious contemplation in London.[39] Yet, in many cases, what were for Bonn elements of a long-term vision were for Paris a rather more immediate, working agenda. Hervé de Charette, France's foreign minister, greeted the Berlin communiqué in ringing terms: 'France is satisfied because for the first time in alliance history, Europe will really be able to express its personality … For the first time we have gone from words to deeds.'[40] But excitement was tinged with caution: 'If this process is completed,' commented de Charette, 'France regards with interest this new Alliance and declares itself ready to participate fully according to a new status.'[41]

France remained as committed as ever to inter-governmentalism in matters of security and defence. Yet, while evidently willing to part company with Germany over the prospects for supranational integration in these fields, France was anxious not to appear a docile convert to the Atlanticist cause. In speeches before the Parliamentary Assembly of the WEU on 3 December 1996, both de Charette and President Chirac affirmed their Europeanist credentials and made it clear that the goal of European cooperation in defence and security was still very much alive.[42] Having declared that, under the new arrangements, the WEU would be the 'vehicle' for ESDI, de Charette foresaw the WEU becoming 'the military wing of the European Union, providing the latter's common foreign and security policy with the military extension it needs to ensure its credibility'. Eventually, the 'logical conclusion' would be that WEU and EU would be brought together, with WEU 'ultimately becoming an integral part of the European Union'. Like de Charette, Chirac posited the 'ultimate insertion of WEU in the Union', but his Euro-enthusiasm exceeded even his foreign minister's. Calling for Europe to 'put an end to its impotence', Chirac professed himself 'as ambitious for Europe in the fields of defence and security as in the economic and political spheres'. The 'first thing', in Chirac's view, would be 'to make the European Council the supreme authority to determine orientation for making decisions in the fields of security and defence'.

France did not, plainly, see the Berlin agreement – in particular the ESDI within NATO formula – as a mere form of words, another fudge to get NATO over a period of tension. France was adamant that the Berlin communiqué, with all its promises, should be implemented, and begin to show results for European security and defence cooperation. The Berlin agreement was therefore merely the starting-point of a process which France would be monitoring closely. And if the promises turned out to be hollow, or the process too long-winded, France reserved the right to halt its *rapprochement* with NATO. On 3 April 1997 – just three months before the Madrid Summit – Chirac delivered a blunt warning that France's new relationship with the Alliance could not be taken for granted: 'If … the Americans intend to maintain complete control of NATO, France will remain in its present situation.'[43] Chirac subsequently carried out his threat at the Madrid Summit by suspending progress in France's *rapprochement* with the Alliance, warning that 'The alliance won't survive durably if there is an unbalanced relationship between Europeans and Americans.'[44]

France's passion for a European 'personality', 'identity' or 'visibility' in defence and security prompted one US official to comment wryly that while the goal-orientated United States was interested in developing the 'S' and 'D' of ESDI, institution-obsessed France was unhealthily preoccupied with the 'I'. More seriously, comments such as those of one French analyst that 'it is necessary to be more Atlanticist today, in order to be more European tomorrow,'[45] fuelled suspicions in Washington that France was manipulating its *rapprochement* with an adapted NATO and the United States in order more rapidly to achieve its Europeanist goals and to boost the European project. French leaders spoke encouragingly of 'the new transatlantic partnership' and of the need for Europe to ensure 'peace and security on its own soil' and 'contribute to world stability', and stressed the importance of the US military commitment to Europe.[46] But they also made it abundantly easy for critics to question their real intentions. When, for example, de Charette stressed the value of 'equilibrium' between European and North American allies, he invited criticism that he was more interested in recovering lost pride (French and European) than in devising better ways for Americans and Europeans to act together militarily. De Charette also saw the object of NATO's adaptation process as to 'give expression to a European identity', whereas in the United States the development of ESDI within NATO was seen as but one part of the new transatlantic partnership. From the point of view of the 'new bargain' analysts in the United States, there was too little evidence that France had escaped the intellectual confines of the Cold War burden-sharing debate, to see the reformed NATO as a means to act in dynamic partnership with the United States, and too little evidence that the French were looking far beyond Europe's own borders.

So there were differences among Europeans, and – at least in France – a seeming inability and/or reluctance to recognize and accept the offer of partnership being made by the United States. American commentators could be excused for thinking that some in Europe were more interested in identities, personalities, expressions and so forth than in doing something concrete in defence and security beyond Europe's borders. The divided and hesitant response of the European allies to the crisis in Zaire in November 1996, and the equally tepid reaction to the collapse of order in Albania in spring 1997, can only have deepened misgivings in Washington.[47]

Europeans on the defensive: prospects for the WEU
'ESDI within NATO' is the formula adopted to bind together Atlanticism and Europeanism in matters of defence and security. Plainly though, there remain differences among the allies over what the formula could – or should – produce. The WEU performs a similar function at the institutional level, in linking NATO with the CFSP of the EU. There are, as with 'ESDI within NATO', sharply different expectations of how, when and for what reason the WEU should develop. But if the delicately crafted Berlin compromise is to be preserved, some means to draw together conflicting political and institutional aspirations for European defence and security will be essential. This section describes the slowly evolving CFSP and asks how well the WEU might satisfy the Europeanist imperative.

The EU, and the European Community before it, is by no means new to practical international politics. With an 'external policy' covering commercial and economic matters, the EU has been 'from its inception an international phenomenon'.[48] There has also been cautious willingness to cooperate (on an informal, ad hoc basis) in more traditional foreign policy areas through the consultation mechanism known as European Political Cooperation (EPC). In time, even the EC Commission became more involved in what was essentially an inter-governmental process. When it was accepted that the Commission could not reasonably be excluded from discussion of foreign economic policy, the October 1981 London Report admitted the Commission to full association with EPC.[49] The 1986 Single European Act gave EPC a basis in EC law and attempted to bring the process closer to the objectives and procedures of the EC. The November 1993 ratification of the Maastricht Treaty on European Union (TEU) replaced EPC with the CFSP, which became one of the three 'pillars' of the new European Union. Some in the Commission, and some member governments, hoped that the TEU would result in a merger of EC and EPC in a 'political union', with a fully integrated foreign and security policy-making machinery,[50] but CFSP remained an inter-governmental process. The Commission's role was enhanced, but cautiously so; the Commission was given a right of initiative in matters of foreign and security policy, but this was not an exclusive right (as in other, EC-driven policy areas) and was to be shared with member governments.[51]

Progress in the development of the CFSP has been slow and often controversial. The CFSP is an inter-governmental pillar, but it also pays homage to the integrationist goals of the European movement. The language of the TEU relied too much upon obscure, inaccessible distinctions between 'foreign', 'security' and 'defence' policies. The result was a very complex and often confusing arrangement (particularly in the process known as 'joint action'), which is usually discussed more in terms of its potential than of its achievement to date: 'As it has developed since [the TEU], CFSP is not a policy, or even a set of policies, but rather a consultation mechanism between governments and EU institutions.'[52] Some see CFSP as merely the depository of peripheral cooperative efforts on the lowest common denominator, while others see it as vitally important to the EU, possibly even the 'cause' which could revitalize and boost the Union into the next century. As it stands, however, the CFSP has very few satisfied followers, and will have to be reformed and improved.[53]

Attempts to nudge CFSP into the world of security and defence have been supervised closely and critically by certain governments, and by early 1997 had achieved relatively little. The mandate for CFSP included 'all questions related to the security of the Union, including the eventual framing of a common defence policy, which might in time lead to a common defence' (TEU Article J.4.1). Yet the flagship of CFSP – the joint action decision-making procedure with the possibility of the use of qualified majority voting for implementation – was not to be applied to defence-related matters: 'Issues having defence implications dealt with under this Article shall not be subject to the [joint-action] procedures set out in Article J.3. (TEU Article J.4.3). The Maastricht Treaty described the WEU as 'an integral part of the development of the Union' (TEU Article J.4.2), and called for it to be developed as 'the defence component of the [EU] and as a means to strengthen the European pillar of the Atlantic Alliance' (TEU, Annex 30). But progress was dismally slow, as was reflected in a December 1994 report on CFSP commissioned by Hans van den Broek, the Commissioner for external political relations. The report condemned the 'inertia and impotence of the CFSP and WEU' as the 'inward and outward reflection of a lack of capacity or will to act, particularly as regards the threat and/or use of force by the Union'. Rather than concede defeat, however, the report robustly (and ambitiously) recommended a 'central capacity for analysis and planning' in all matters relating to CFSP and defence, and commented on the 'twin perils of blinkered concentration on hastily conceived "joint actions" on the one hand and sterile bureaucratisation on the other'.[54]

After this slow start, performance in 1995 was little better, at least in the view of the European Parliament (EP). The EP has the right, under TEU Article J.7, to hold an annual debate on the implementation of the

CFSP. The EP's May 1996 report covered the second of these debates, referring to the implementation of CFSP in 1995.[55] The EP was deeply unimpressed. On the subject of the relationship between CFSP and a Common Defence Policy (CDP) and Common Defence (CD), the EP argued that 'progress in framing a common defence policy and developing a European security system, in which the EU has a central role to play, is essential to the Union if it is to have an effective CFSP in the coming years ... without a common defence policy and a common system of deterrence the Union will never be able to implement a CFSP.' Yet the record of achievement in 1995 was not good. The EP found 'little development of the CFSP instruments and such precarious progress towards the framing of a common defence policy', and judged that 'the implementation of the CFSP took a step backward in 1995.'

The EP report was passed to the Commission for information, and it may have been this document which prompted a sober reassessment of the potential of CFSP by DGIA, the Commission directorate leading on CFSP matters. In a briefing paper issued the following month, DGIA appeared willing to accept more modest goals for CFSP (a less charitable interpretation would be that it was grasping at straws): CFSP was still useful as a foreign policy mechanism, but more as the legal basis for financing and implementing UN Security Council sanctions, for example, than as an instrument of policy-making; Commission input into CFSP should be preserved, and in this vein the idea of a Presidency/ Commission 'tandem' might maintain the 'visibility' of the CFSP; finally, DGIA wanted qualified majority voting to be the norm for CFSP except in military matters, which was prevented by the TEU.[56] Some months later, a Commission official closely involved in the CFSP accepted that the TEU's 'high hopes' for a CFSP 'have not been realised'.[57]

Whatever his reservations about the implementation of CFSP, Hans van den Broek had no time for Cassandras – even among his own officials. In early May 1996 the Commissioner was to be found arguing for a more prominent 'European' role in matters of defence and security, particularly as regards the follow-on to IFOR in Bosnia. Van den Broek's proposal, it was reported, 'would imply a sharp acceleration in the EU's so far tortuous efforts to develop a fully-fledged foreign and security policy, and it is likely to provoke intensive debate on both sides of the Atlantic'.[58] The most revealing aspect of this episode, however, is that 'intensive debate' was *not* provoked; the proposal seemed to sink without trace in the approach to the WEU and NATO meetings which followed soon after. When WEU foreign and defence ministers met in

Birmingham on 7 May 1996 they stressed the need to develop the WEU's operational capabilities which they saw as 'a prerequisite for an effective and credible European defence capability *to carry out the Petersberg tasks*'.[59] From the WEU's point of view, therefore, a 'Europe-only' follow-on to IFOR in Bosnia, on the scale necessary, could not be a real possibility for some time to come. But, for the 'van den Broek school', there was worse to come. The following month, speaking after the Berlin NATO ministerial, Britain's Foreign Secretary was of the view that the WEU's new role 'did not include combat missions'.[60] And the EU was hardly noticed during the June NATO meetings; both the foreign and defence ministers' communiqués made many references to ESDI, the 'Euro-Atlantic area' and 'European allies', but barely one reference to the EU. WEU officials and supporters, on the other hand, are fond of pointing out that the Berlin communiqué refers to the WEU a flattering 29 times.

A polite scepticism usually surrounds discussion of the EU's capacity to organize its own security and defence. Yet in spite of this, it is hard to imagine either the complete marginalization of the EU in Europe's new security architecture, or a NATO-derived European defence 'identity' which, averse to combat, had all the military significance of an air ambulance and over which the EU would have no real political control beyond the capacity to 'request' the WEU to conduct this or that operation. There is much in the 1996 Brussels agreement to make independent-minded Europeans uneasy, particularly the extent to which the 'new' NATO, its operations and even those of the WEU will be controlled and shaped by Washington. And there is still a good deal of momentum behind the formal development of the defence and security aspects of CFSP. With CDP and CD established as 'eventual' EU goals in the Maastricht Treaty, the 1996–7 IGC could hardly have avoided discussion of security and defence issues. Media coverage of the IGC discussion was thin, but the following issues were among those being debated in and around the conference:

- the Swedish/Finnish proposal to include the WEU's Petersberg humanitarian and rescue tasks as EU treaty commitments;
- whether political control of a 'European' CJTF should be in the hands of the EU's Council of Ministers rather than the WEU's;
- whether an EU 'request' for WEU military action should necessarily go through a second ministerial filter at the WEU;

- the introduction of a 'flexibility clause' to allow some members to proceed (in specific actions or in general integration), while others opt for 'constructive abstention';
- the modification of decision-making processes to reduce the emphasis on consensus;
- whether, in time, the WEU should be folded completely into the EU.

Given that there is substantial opposition in Europe to the suggestion of an EU defence expression outside NATO and a merger of the WEU and EU,[61] and that the principal interest of the IGC was in devising ways and means for the EU to expand eastwards, it would have been unwise to expect much movement on CFSP at the Amsterdam Summit. The final stages of the IGC descended into acrimony and the outcome – the 'Draft Treaty of Amsterdam' – was the subject of ridicule even before it appeared.[62] The document was poorly drafted and muddled in many places, to the irritation of several EU governments.[63] There would, plainly be a great deal of work to do before a final text of the treaty could be signed by governments towards the end of 1997. But as far as CFSP is concerned, and subject to any further amendments, the member states set themselves goals arguably more cautious and modest than those declared in the TEU, and were evidently anxious to retain the inter-governmental character of CFSP:

> The [CFSP] shall include all questions relating to the security of the Union, including the *progressive* framing of a common defence policy . . . which might in time lead to a common defence, *should the European Council so decide*. It shall in that case recommend to the Member States the adoption of such a decision *in accordance with their respective constitutional requirements*. ... The Union shall ... foster closer institutional relations with the WEU with a view to the *possibility* of the integration of the WEU into the Union, *should the European Council so decide*.[64]

A protocol on 'enhanced cooperation' between the EU and WEU would be drawn up. As far as the scope of EU/WEU military missions was concerned, the draft treaty accepted that these would be towards the lower end of the spectrum: 'humanitarian and rescue tasks, peacekeeping tasks and tasks of combat forces in crisis management, including peace-making'.[65]

The quality and future of CFSP are still uncertain. This makes it difficult to judge how well the WEU could serve the Europeanist ideal, and
difficult therefore to know whether – and for how long – the WEU could
satisfy the need for a lubricant between the EU and NATO. Nevertheless,
the WEU has been very active, developing its organizational and operational capability and improving its relations with NATO and the EU.[66]
After the renaissance of the Brussels Treaty in the mid-1950s, the WEU
was reinvigorated for the second time by the Rome Declaration of
October 1984, largely to improve Europe's showing in the transatlantic
burden-sharing debate. Yet, in spite of confident assertions made then,
and in the October 1987 Hague Platform, the forum continued to languish
in relative obscurity for some years.[67] In 1991, however, when WEU members annexed their declaration to the Maastricht Treaty, the WEU became
a full member of the post-Cold War European security debating society.

Since 1992 the WEU has conducted several small-scale military and
policing operations and is preparing for more. A WEU Planning Cell,
with an Intelligence Section and a Situation Centre, has been established
in Brussels at WEU headquarters. The organization is developing its
satellite intelligence centre at Torrejon in Spain. WEU staff have drawn
up lists of WEU-answerable forces, and are examining the case for a
WEU 'Humanitarian Task Force'. WEU planning staff have prepared
draft contingency plans, as well as a Strategic Mobility Concept to
facilitate Petersberg missions. US critics might therefore be reassured
that their European allies *are* thinking beyond their own territorial
defence. In December 1995 the WEU began its own 12-month command
post exercise – CRISEX 95/96 – in which the WEU was notionally
mandated by the UN (though not 'requested' by the EU) to ensure safe
delivery of humanitarian aid to a fictional country.

Political and military relations between WEU and NATO have also
been improved, with a long-awaited mechanism for exchange of classified
documents being agreed in May 1996, and with regular meetings between
WEU and NATO civilian and military staff.[68] Having contributed several
papers to NATO's CJTF consultation process, the WEU passed six
contingency plans for a WEU-led CJTF to NATO; by spring 1997,
NATO's military planners had completed work on two of these plans.
NATO's first full CJTF exercise is scheduled for 1998, and the Alliance
has promised that the second CJTF exercise will trial one of the WEU
options. Other NATO/WEU command post exercises are being
considered for 2000 and beyond. The EU has also been the target of
WEU affections. In late 1993 the EU and WEU Councils agreed various

cooperative measures such as a mechanism for the exchange of unclassified information, harmonization of meeting dates, venues and work programmes, and limited attendance at each other's meetings.

Relations between the WEU and the European Commission were also developed. In October 1994 the General Affairs Council of the EU made its first formal *request* to the WEU for assistance, leading to WEU management of the international policing of Mostar. During 1995 the WEU also contributed a paper to the IGC preparatory phase. More broadly, the WEU also makes an important contribution to western outreach to central and eastern Europe through its Associate Partnership scheme, and provides a convenient base for the EU's former neutral states as they move tentatively towards more formal membership of a European defence and security order. The WEU has therefore achieved a great deal in a short time – and, furthermore, with a staff of fewer than 300 and a budget of about £28 million: roughly 4 per cent that of NATO.

The WEU is clearly developing a significant, if small-scale, staff-operational capability, and its political profile and value have been increasing steadily. Some questions remain about the WEU's relations with NATO (the document exchange agreement, for example, has its limitations), and about the precise way in which a WEU-led CJTF would be equipped, conducted, monitored and concluded (although by spring 1997 one senior US official was describing these arrangements as '99 per cent' complete). There may also be doubts about the propriety and wisdom of this development, given the possibility that small-scale operations could expand and that the WEU still has at its core Article 5 of the modified Brussels Treaty; a wholly unambiguous collective defence commitment.[69] And without a firmer impression of the prospects for CFSP, it is next to impossible to judge the WEU against its most important task, namely, that of using the agreed ESDI-within-NATO formula to build a convincing relationship between the Atlanticists and the Europeanists. Whatever the reservations, however, the WEU should at least make possible a working compromise between these two approaches to European security, and between integrationism and inter-governmentalism as styles of cooperation. There is, *prima facie*, no reason to suppose that the WEU will *not* serve CFSP adequately, as and when CFSP develops. And it may even be, to take up the argument used by the European Parliament and others, that the WEU could hasten the development and consolidation of CFSP.

Much is therefore possible, and in practical – rather than theoretical – terms, little if anything has been foreclosed. The developing Euro-

Atlantic security relationship will, however, hold only for as long as the WEU remains an integral and visible part of it. WEU does have the appearance, and some of the substance, of a European security and defence institution, but its main role is to lubricate the relationship between NATO and the EU, for as long as these institutions differ in their membership and role. Without increased political, military and above all financial commitment from west European governments, it is hard to envisage the WEU becoming a coherent, self-contained amd militarily effective alliance, rather than merely an (admittedly vital) political expedient. And it is equally hard to see such commitments being made while defence budgets are being constrained so severely throughout western Europe. Everything might, of course, change. Washington might develop a plan, say, to leave Europe to its own defence and security by 2005. NATO might then lose its 'O', becoming a more general, Article 2-style, political and cultural forum than a military alliance. The CFSP might somehow be made more dynamic and ambitious and be accepted across the EU as a sound basis for a CDP and CD. In either circumstance, and provided the awkward matter of declining defence budgets could be addressed, then the WEU might – and might have to – be transformed into a genuine defence and security alliance or 'component' of the EU. But for the foreseeable future, the compromise agreed at the June 1996 Berlin ministerial seems likely to prevail, with the WEU acting as a crucial *passe-partout* in the overall European defence and security framework.[70]

The defence industry

Beyond the observation that the manufacture, supply and maintenance of military equipment and weapons could reasonably form part of *any* discussion of military operations, there are more pressing reasons to address the defence industry in the context of the post-Cold War trans-atlantic security relationship. If, for example, North American and European allies are becoming more willing to contemplate 'coalitions of the able and willing' to manage this or that crisis in Europe or beyond, then interoperability and standardization of military equipment will remain important issues in the years ahead. A coalition which relies on one or a few sources of equipment should be militarily more efficient than one which deploys a multitude of exotic and incompatible weapon types and C^4I) systems. If the coalition expects to form and deploy rapidly, then the level of standardization could prove to be vital to the success of the operation, and may lead to some states being excluded as 'willing' but regrettably not 'able'. There is a case, therefore, for a regime of trans-atlantic defence industrial cooperation to underpin the institutional coop-eration currently being put in place, however hesitantly. Without such cooperation, and with scarce resources supporting too many manufactur-ing outlets, the fledgling achievements at the political/institutional level could be undermined by competition for export markets between a US and a west European defence industrial bloc: 'Ferocious competition between Europe and the United States for arms sales on world markets threatens to undermine the military foundation of the alliance – the ability of NATO's 16 member nations to fight together with compatible weap-onry.'[71] As in the broader security relationship, the allies are required to perform a delicate balancing act; each side must be allowed to follow its own course (in this case defence industrial consolidation) while at the same time pursuing the goals of transatlantic cooperation. And it may even be – as with institutional cooperation – that a certain level and style of defence industrial consolidation (and therefore exclusivity) on the part of the European allies could make for a stronger and more cooperative transatlantic relationship.

During the Cold War defence industrial cooperation, competition and market access were constant features of the transatlantic security partnership, particularly in the context of the burden-sharing debate. A great number of initiatives were launched, variously on a Euro-NATO, European, or NATO-wide basis. Eurogroup was set up in 1968 by European NATO states (France and Iceland were not members) as a forum for defence ministers. The main focus was on defence support services such as training, logistics, communications and medicine. In the shadow of the Nixon Doctrine and the threat to withdraw US troops from Europe, Eurogroup spawned the European Defence Improvement Pro-gramme (EDIP) which ran from 1970 to 1975. The idea of EDIP was to enable European NATO members to take on a larger slice of NATO's defence burden in Europe. Between 1992 and 1994 Eurogroup transferred its functions to NATO and the WEU. Eurogroup passed into history on 1 January 1994, the only remnant being the 'Eurodinner', a meeting of European defence ministers on the eve of NATO's annual DPC meeting.[72] (For the time being, of course, the ministers must continue to forgo a French menu.)

Non-NATO European cooperation was exemplified by the Independ-ent European Programme Group (IEPG), founded in 1976 by 13 European members of NATO (including France and Turkey but excluding Iceland).

The mandate was to promote cooperation in European defence R&D and production with a view to competing more effectively against US industry. In autumn 1988 the IEPG produced an 'Action plan on a stepwise development of a European armaments market'. The main recommendations of the action plan were open competition and cross-border bidding, and a system of *juste retour* for participants in a joint contract. The IEPG also created the European Cooperative Long-term Initiative for Defence (Euclid), an attempt to coordinate defence R&D among IEPG members.[73] In December 1992 IEPG ministers agreed to transfer the functions of the IEPG to the embryonic Western European Armaments Group (WEAG).

NATO-wide initiatives included the Long-Term Defence Programme (LTDP) and the stilted development of the 'two-way street' in defence manufacturing, competition and procurement. In 1977 NATO members agreed to increase annual defence spending by 3 per cent over inflation. The purpose of the LTDP was to ensure that the increase was spent wisely. There were ten main areas of concern: readiness; reinforcement; reserve mobilization; maritime forces; air defence; C^3; electronic warfare; standardization and interoperability; logistics; and theatre nuclear force modernization. The 'two-way street' – a particular concern of NATO's Conference of National Armaments Directors (CNAD) since the late 1980s – was an attempt to develop a more productive and cooperative atmosphere, with a politically binding Code of Conduct for intra-Alliance defence trade.

Taken together, these initiatives – along with those reflected in a host of other acronyms – give some idea of the stress which has long been laid on defence industrial matters in the broader US–European security partnership. They also suggest, by their diversity and abundance, that the task of balancing cooperation with competition in defence industry has been especially challenging. The CNAD initiative, for example, proceeded 'slowly' and 'cantankerously' into the 1990s,[74] and the same might be said of the transatlantic defence industrial relationship as a whole.

After the Cold War, existing unease in the transatlantic defence industrial relationship has been deepened by dramatic reductions in defence spending in Europe and North America. Across NATO, defence spending fell by some US$88 billion between 1985 and 1995 (at 1995 prices) – a reduction of about 16 per cent for the Alliance as a whole. Of that total, about US$12 billion (13 per cent) of the decrease is attributable to NATO's European allies, who together reduced their defence spending by about 6 per cent over the decade. Some 85 per cent of the reduction was made in the United States, where defence spending dropped by about

US\$75 billion; a remarkable 21 per cent reduction over the decade.[75] Savings have been made across the board: armed forces have reduced their manpower and, in some cases, have abandoned conscription; training budgets have been cut; and overseas bases have been closed. The procurement of weapons, military equipment and stores has been reduced considerably, and the funding of defence-related research and development has also felt the pinch. All this suggests that the prospects for transatlantic defence industrial cooperation – limited enough during the Cold War times of plenty – may in fact be dwindling. Furthermore if, as this rudimentary statistical analysis suggests, US defence industries have borne a disproportionate amount of NATO's spending cuts, there may be even less willingness in future to accept European penetration of US domestic and international markets in the name of transatlantic harmony, and more readiness to see European defence industry as a hostile competitor.[76]

Since the end of the Cold War defence industry across NATO, faced with sharply reduced orders, has been in nothing short of a crisis. The response has generally been to consolidate in order to be able better to compete for national, regional and international markets. Consolidation of the defence industrial base in the United States has been dramatic in both speed and scale. Between 1992 and late 1996 the number of major US defence businesses fell from 32 to just nine, with several other mergers and acquisitions in the pipeline. Three industrial giants have emerged. The merger of Lockheed and Martin Marietta in 1995, and their acquisition of Loral in 1996, produced the world's biggest defence company; Lockheed Martin's defence sales in 1995 were worth US\$19.39 billion. In July 1997 it was announced that the unstoppable Lockheed Martin had agreed to merge with Northrop Grumman, taking the group's defence sales to about US\$25bn (1995 figures).[77] Boeing's acquisition of Rockwell's defence interests and, most recently, McDonnell Douglas has created the world's largest integrated aerospace company, with overall (i.e.defence and civil) revenues for 1997 projected to soar to about US\$50 billion.[78] Finally, the merger of Raytheon with Hughes Electronics and the military division of Texas Instruments will produce a conglomerate with defence revenues equivalent to US\$11.67 billion, on 1995 calculations.[79]

European defence industries have also long recognized that their manufacturing capacity is far in excess of what their customers might need, nationally or regionally, and there has been a pronounced industry-led effort to consolidate the European defence industrial base since the end of the Cold War. US consolidation has added another element of urgency to the European effort. A simple comparison of the European and US defence sectors illustrates the point. With a total procurement budget only half the size of that of the United States, Europe's defence sector nevertheless has more prime contractors than in the United States, in all major sectors including armoured vehicles, warships and fighter aircraft. The result is that US defence manufacturers, even if they were to look no further than their domestic market, enjoy economies of scale not found in Europe; and these economies of scale, of course, suggest that US firms will not be content with the US market but will exploit their advantage in foreign markets, including Europe. European industry must therefore consolidate, both to reflect the reduced European market and to ensure that it can compete with US industry for European and global orders.

Defence industrial consolidation in Europe has, however, been 'painfully slow' and on a much smaller scale.[80] Europe's four biggest defence firms – British Aerospace, Thomson and Aérospatiale/Dassault of France and the UK's GEC – had revenues in 1995 of US$6.47 billion, US$4.68 billion, US$4.15 billion and US$4.12 billion respectively.[81] If European defence industries are to compete on near-equal terms with their US counterparts, then large-scale consolidation must take place across Europe. But even if this were possible, European manufacturers would still have to fight hard. The Raytheon/Hughes/Texas Instruments combination stands to dominate the world missile market, with sales of about US$5 billion per annum. If all eleven European guided missile manufacturing firms could consolidate into one, their total revenue would still only be in the region of US$4 billion.[82] Certainly, the European defence industry is no stranger to cross-border mergers and acquisitions, or to either commercially led or inter-governmental joint ventures, but the consolidation process is still in its infancy and has not yet produced anything to match the US giants.

Defence industrial consolidation in the United States has all along been encouraged by the US government. In Europe, however, in spite of pressure from industry to consolidate, the inability or unwillingness of governments to loosen control of national defence sectors has had a restraining effect. Compared with the United States, European consolidation therefore has an extra obstacle to cross, and the inability of key governments to agree on the style and purpose of consolidation suggests that a 'European defence industrial base' will be more of an aspiration than a reality for some time to come. There have been several initiatives at the inter-governmental and institutional levels, but so far the results have been disappointing. In November 1996, after years of often acrimonious debate, the Franco-German Armaments Agency admitted Britain and Italy as new members and was renamed the Joint Armaments Cooperation Organization (JACO), mandated to coordinate research, development and manufacture among the four members. One week later, the stunted Western European Armaments Group was transformed into two new WEU-sponsored bodies: the Western European Armaments Organization (WEAO: responsible for coordinating research) and the Western European Armaments Agency (WEAA: designed to manage common procurement projects among WEU members). This sudden proliferation of organizations struck some commentators and industrialists as ill-advised and confusing, particularly given the uncertain relationship between JACO and the new WEU bodies. The new constellation of European armaments institutions was aptly described by one transatlantic commentator as 'a dog's breakfast' when it was revealed to the world,[83] and prompts the question whether the WEU is being as helpful in the US–European defence industrial relationship as it is in the broader transatlantic security dialogue.

The prospects for European defence consolidation and its effects on the broader US–European security relationship can be described loosely in terms of the Europeanist and Atlanticist approaches discussed elsewhere in this paper. In the first place, European governments could pursue the development of cross-border 'Euro-champions', supported by a 'Europe-first' procurement policy. This would not necessarily preclude cooperation with US firms, and could be an effective way to lever fully reciprocal market access. The result could be a US–European defence industrial relationship which, while inherently volatile, would nevertheless be fairly robust and based on mutual respect. The 'Atlanticist' approach to defence industry would prefer consolidation into national champions which could then cooperate with either European or North American industries as circumstances and the market dictated. Following the French government's rejection of GEC-Marconi's bid for Thomson-CSF (and its subsequent decision to postpone the privatization of Thomson), and with the possibility that BAe and GEC will combine, rather than continue the quest for cross-border mergers in Europe,[84] it may be that some defence manufacturers have already embarked upon (or been compelled to adopt) this approach, which could have certain benefits for the overall US–European relationship. Particularly as the wisdom of the 'America first' policy comes under increased scrutiny in the United States, transatlantic defence industrial cooperation and even integration could create a web of interdependence which underpins the evolving security relationship. Combined US–European military operations could be more spontaneous and effective as equipment and weapon standardization improves. Finally, a potentially bitter and divisive competition among US and European companies to supply the newly opening markets of central and eastern Europe could be avoided.[85] By one assessment, the Czech Republic, Hungary and Poland may soon have a combined requirement for 150 fighter aircraft: 'theirs could be one of the largest arms buys in the world, totalling more than $3 billion and carrying long-term consequences for spare parts, maintenance and industrial cooperation.'[86]

In defence industrial terms, both 'Europeanism' and 'Atlanticism' offer benefits for the broader US–European relationship. But there are also risks to consider. The creation and support of Euro-champions could be seen as brash and confrontational – rather than the stuff of which partnerships are made – by US industry, public and Congress. The result could be a particularly cruel struggle to secure global market share. The disadvantage of the 'Atlanticist' approach is that national champions in Europe might still find it hard to compete with the US giants. The European defence industry would therefore be accepting a conciliatory and even subservient position in respect of its US counterpart. Nevertheless, if both the United States and the European allies genuinely seek a transatlantic partnership underpinned by healthy cooperation and competition in defence industrial matters, then either Europeanism or Atlanticism could be a reasonable course to follow. If, on the other hand, partnership is not the real object, or is at best a temporary means to some other end, then in both cases the risks will very soon be perceived to outweigh the benefits and cooperation will be undermined.

Conclusion

This chapter set out to probe for weaknesses in the arrangements reached at Berlin in June 1996 and elaborated over the following 15 months. There may, over time, prove to be three such weaknesses. The first concerns differing perceptions among US and European allies over the character and significance of any agreements reached so far. Among the many different opinions on US–European security dealings held by the US public and Congress and within the foreign and defence policy-making machinery, there is a new and widespread feeling that the Cold War burden-sharing issue has had its day and must be replaced by something altogether more outward-looking and progressive. The transatlantic security relationship can no longer be centred upon the Soviet threat. The 'glue' of a new, post-Cold War US–European *partnership* must be shared values and interests, a similar vision of the future, and a shared feeling of responsibility. The United States must be the leader in this partnership. But rather than relying upon its wealth and military might to lead as a benevolent hegemon, the United States expects a new form of consensual leadership: the European allies must *want* to be led and supported and must *want* to contribute to the *combined* effort. The US–European partnership, no longer defined by external pressures, must be driven from within, by a sense of fellow feeling and kinship; as one US official quipped, 'just tell us that you love us.' If the European allies fail – or refuse – to acknowledge these misgivings then it is difficult to foresee a flourishing partnership with the United States.

Part of being 'outward-looking and progressive' involves shaking off the Cold War preoccupation with European territorial security and defence. There are signs, however, that the European allies have not kept pace with the United States in this regard. There are other indications that some European allies have interpreted the Berlin agreement in terms which would be neither understood nor welcomed in the United States, particularly over whether, how and when the ESDI-within-NATO formula should contribute to the development of a discretely European defence and security 'identity'. It is here that the real problem of differing perceptions becomes clear. There has never, since 1945, been a flawless 'transatlantic consensus', and no official, politician or analyst could have expected the Berlin communiqué to have resolved all US–European differences for all time. Transatlantic disagreement has been, and will remain, normal, and may even be a force for good within the Alliance. The problem, instead, is that there are important differences of opinion among the European allies. This has also been a feature of Alliance politics for decades. But whereas during the Cold War the domineering United States may have welcomed divisions among its European allies – *divide et impera (amice)* – such divisions are now more likely to be seen as an impediment to an effective, outwardly oriented partnership.

Intra-European disagreements are often expressed in institutional terms, giving rise to the common misgiving in the United States that the European allies have lost sight of the purpose of security cooperation, while becoming obsessed with its external appearance.[87] European security institutions and their interrelations also point to the second potential weakness in the new US–European security partnership. Part of the partnership is an elaborate relationship among three institutions: NATO on one side, the European Union on the other and the WEU in the middle holding the whole edifice together (at least until other foundations can be built). The flaw is not necessarily that the relationship is too complex and unwieldy, but that one element (the EU's view of itself as a security and defence player) is still developing. The transatlantic security partnership, as developed during 1996 and 1997, requires the EU to grow as a security and defence actor within certain constraints. If those constraints are ignored or, indeed, if sufficient growth does not take place, then the partnership (as currently devised) can only falter.

The state of transatlantic defence industrial cooperation is the third weakness in the evolving US–European partnership. Equal access to national markets and procurement systems, the pace and scope of consolidation, cross-border and transatlantic mergers and acquisitions, and competition for global market share are all issues upon which the United States and its European allies could disagree bitterly in the near future. Yet, once again, it is more than mere disagreement which could weaken the partnership; defence procurement and equipment standardization have long been thorns in NATO's side. Much more serious would be the failure to recognize that disagreement must be managed if the partnership is to endure. To argue either that 'market forces must decide', or that the defence industry is a strategic national asset which must be protected, is to accept that however much the allies may wish to collaborate, this core element of defence and security cooperation will be marked more by disharmony. And without the urgency, common purpose and discipline of the Cold War, it is difficult to see what could prevent the spread of the rottenness at the core.

Chapter 6

Conclusion

'If we resort to an indirect test, and ask Nature 'Who are the fittest: those [species] who are continually at war with each other, or those who support one another?' we at once see that those animals which acquire habits of mutual aid are undoubtedly the fittest.'
— PRINCE PETER KROPOTKIN, *MUTUAL AID: A FACTOR IN EVOLUTION*

This paper has attempted to assess the health of NATO, the embodiment of the US–European defence and security relationship. The analysis proceeds from the premise that, whatever else the transatlantic alliance may do in the near or medium-term future (such as admit the Czech Republic, Hungary, Poland and possibly other members), without a sound partnership and a vision shared by the United States and its long-standing west European allies, the alliance which proved so durable during the Cold War will soon become obsolete, or at least change out of all recognition.

This paper has therefore put analysis of NATO's internal adaptation before consideration of the causes and consequences of outreach and enlargement. That said, the 'internal' and 'external' aspects of change cannot sensibly be separated. The complexity and controversy of the internal adaptation programme doubtless contributed to the decision to admit just a small number of new members in the first tranche. And when (or, just possibly, if) the chosen three become full members of the Alliance, NATO's new force posture, the CJTF, the command structure and perhaps even a new strategy will all need to be tested rigorously. Of particular interest in the years ahead will be the respective priority accorded to Article 5 and non-Article 5 contingencies, and NATO's ability to respond effectively in each category.

Conclusion

This study inclines towards a mixture of optimism, incrementalism and caution when contemplating NATO's future. As such, it is probably too accepting of Cold War-style thinking and institutional inertia. There is another, rather more adventurous view: that the Alliance's best hope for survival into the next millennium is to shed its past and grasp at change, however dramatic and unsettling, shaping the agenda in its own interests. But since its own history is one of the few things NATO can be sure of at present, and since it is in the nature of military alliances to be conservative, evolution seems more appropriate than revolution. NATO, and the broader European security debate, must continue to evolve to keep pace with change. Metaphorically, the search is on for a car which combines the safety and reliability of a spacious family estate with the speed, responsiveness and appeal of a sports car. The search may not be in vain; Volvo have, after all, managed against all the odds to produce a glamorous estate car.[1] The central conclusion of this paper is that the Volvo model can be applied to military alliances; a cautious, conservative but imaginative approach to the transatlantic security relationship could in time enable the United States and its European allies to feel excitingly safe.

The 1990s have not been the easiest of times for the US–European defence and security relationship. An elaborate and imaginative compromise was engineered between the June 1996 NATO ministerial meeting in Berlin and the July 1997 summit meeting in Madrid. Several key elements of that compromise remain, however, to be agreed; and the compromise as a whole has yet to be tested *in extremis*, politically and militarily. The 'new', adapted NATO could yet face severe challenges from within. Furthermore, disagreements during the ratification phase of the enlargement process could undermine the Alliance severely. And unless the European Union's CFSP is given sufficient momentum, enabling the WEU to fulfil the role set for it, the politically and militarily vital – but no less fragile – ESDI-within-NATO formula will almost certainly fail to fulfil its promise.

These policy difficulties aside, a still deeper concern is that the Alliance may not yet have convinced its members, its critics or indeed itself that it has found a clear enough mission. Worse still, the absence, now and for the foreseeable future, of a large-scale external threat may mean that a clear mission will *never* be found. In these circumstances, the United States and its European allies may find themselves trying to base their defence and security relationship not on mutually perceived danger but on a mixture of historical sentimentality and a vaguely perceived duty

113

to manage crises and low-intensity conflicts around the world. During the Cold War, there was ample reason for a close-knit US–European alliance, and no practical alternative to it. After the Cold War, the need for such an alliance is less obvious, and possible alternatives to it are contemplated more readily.

At several points in this book, the evolving NATO has been likened to a 'virtual' alliance, one which focuses on tasks and capabilities rather than threats and territories, and which will be available and effective when needed (but not before). Alexander Vershbow, adviser to President Clinton, made the following assessment of NATO adaptation: 'The ultimate success of the NATO alliance will depend not on capabilities and institutional innovations alone, but on the unity and cohesion of the alliance and the willingness of its members to act for a common purpose *when circumstances require.*'[2] With a glimmer of sarcasm, one British official sensed the arrival of a new 'doctrine of extreme re-configurability', whereby a machine is assembled only for as long as it is needed, and is then dismantled. 'Extreme re-configurability' poses two problems. The first is that it amounts to the institutionalization of ad hoc cooperation; a concept sufficiently self-contradictory to present an interesting intellectual and practical challenge for Alliance policy-makers and officials. The second problem is that, for the sake of cohesion and flexibility, NATO may have been forced to remodel itself in such a way – enabling 'coalitions of the able and willing' – that Alliance cohesion may be *less* rather than *more* likely in a future non-vital politico-military crisis.

There are, plainly, flaws in the 'new' NATO, giving grounds to question the durability of the transatlantic security relationship. Some of these flaws are mere points of detail that will be resolved relatively easily. Others are more fundamental and structural differences which, unless managed carefully, could seriously undermine the Alliance. But there are also more positive signs. The first is that in such harsh conditions, the fact that NATO has not yet succumbed – to the satisfaction of the vultures circling overhead – is proof of a certain resilience. NATO is a determined survivor; the transatlantic security relationship may be beset by problems, some of them of a fundamental nature, but this is hardly news. It might be inferred, particularly from chapter 5, that NATO has sought to be all things to all its members, in an unsatisfactory scheme which is bound to come unstuck. But a more optimistic interpretation could be made. The fact that each of the main NATO members could emerge from the June 1996 ministerial claiming the communiqué as a victory for its own national position could be seen as a triumph for a complex organization seeking to find its way in uncertain times. Some have also argued that, in spite of all the rhetoric, the internal adaptation of the Alliance represents only a token gesture in the direction of the 'Europeanization' of NATO or the development of a discretely European security and defence 'identity'. But, in response, it is difficult to see how something as insubstantial as ESDI could have been recognized and accommodated in any other, more tangible way.

In the introductory chapter it was suggested that institutions, for all their conservatism, can act as a framework which *encourages* change rather than recoils from it. But no international institution – not even one with the most complex, survival-oriented bureaucracy – could survive for long without members. If the transatlantic security institution is to survive and remain useful, the member states of NATO must at some point decide that the relationship is *prima facie* worth the effort and that it can be used to address evolving security challenges. The United States and its European allies do not *have* to make this decision, but they cannot expect their institution to motivate and lead itself. Without the coherence and shared purpose imposed by an external threat, all that remains as the basis for the transatlantic security partnership is a general vote of confidence of this sort; NATO has become an 'alliance of choice', rather than an 'alliance of necessity'. This is hardly the most stable foundation, and it is one which will require constantly to be checked and reinforced, but without it there can be no institution. For the Europeanists and Atlanticists alike, a vote of confidence in this evolving institution would be a rational decision. The compromise agreed at Berlin in June 1996 and developed thereafter is one which deals with the present without closing off other options, including the future development of a European 'identity'. History may even show that the development of the European Union as a fully fledged security and defence institution – if it is to go down this path – had as much to do with the 'bottom-up' spill-over from NATO's internal adaptation as with the 'top-down', declaratory approach of the EU's Council of Ministers.

The US–European security relationship is, remarkably enough, not too unhealthy. ~~The prognosis is therefore good, although full recovery from the end of the Cold War will be delayed for as long as the patient~~

The prognosis is therefore good, although full recovery from the end of the Cold War will be delayed for as long as the patient chooses not to believe diagnosis.

Notes

Chapter 1: Introduction: the US–European security partnership after the Cold War

1 T. Flockhart makes a useful distinction between 'outreach' (being pleasant to former adversaries, for example) and 'enlargement' (acceding formally to a treaty), both of which are subsets of the 'dynamics of [NATO, WEU, EU] expansion': 'The Dynamics of Expansion: NATO, WEU, EU', *European Security* (5/2, Summer 1996), pp. 196–7.

2 'Patching up NATO', *The Economist*, 19 November 1994.

3 S. Sloan, 'US Perspectives on NATO's Future', *International Affairs* (71/2, April 1995), p. 229.

4 R.A. Manning, 'Futureshock or Renewed Partnership? The US–Japan Alliance Facing the Millennium', *Washington Quarterly* (18/4, Autumn 1995), p. 87.

5 P.J. Garrity and S.K. Weiner, 'U.S. Defense Strategy after the Cold War', in B. Roberts (ed.), *US Security in an Uncertain Era* (Cambridge, Mass.: MIT Press, 1993), pp. 32–3.

6 J. Solana, 'NATO in Transition', *Perceptions: Journal of International Affairs* (1/1, 1996), p. 9.

7 P. Zelikow, 'The Masque of Institutions', *Survival* (38/1, Spring 1996), p. 7.

8 V. Rühe, text of address to the Royal Institute of International Affairs and the Konrad-Adenauer-Stiftung, Chatham House, 19 November 1996.

Chapter 2: Military alliances in theory

1 D.G. Haglund, 'Must NATO Fail?', *International Journal* (50/4, Autumn 1995), p. 665.

2 Ibid., p. 656.

3 R.B. McCalla, 'NATO's Persistence after the Cold War', *International Organization* (50/3, Summer 1996), p. 447.
4 S.M. Walt, *The Origins of Alliances* (Ithaca and London: Cornell University Press, 1987), p. 5.
5 Ibid., p. 17.
6 K.N. Waltz, 'The New World Order', *Millennium: Journal of International Relations* (22/2, 1993), p. 189. See also K.N. Waltz, 'The Emerging Structure of International Politics', *International Security* (18/2, Fall 1993).
7 'Germany's Wooing of Uneasy Russia Unsettles Nerves in Central Europe', *The Times*, 7 February 1996.
8 S.P. Huntington, 'The Clash of Civilizations?', *Foreign Affairs* (72/3, Summer 1993).
9 A. Toynbee, *The World and the West* (Oxford: Oxford University Press, 1953).
10 Huntington, 'The Clash of Civilizations?', p. 23.
11 *The Atlantic Alliance's Strategic Concept* (Brussels: NATO, November 1991), paras 8ff.
12 W. Claes, 'NATO's Agenda for a New European Order', *Financial Times*, 23 February 1995.
13 See F. Ajami, 'The Summoning', and K. Mahbubani, 'The Dangers of Decadence: What the Rest Can Teach the West', in *Foreign Affairs* (72/4, September/October 1993).
14 See S.P. Huntington, 'If Not Civilizations, What? Paradigms of the Post-Cold War World', *Foreign Affairs* (72/5, November/December 1993).
15 S.P. Huntington, 'The West: Unique, Not Universal', *Foreign Affairs* (75/6, November/December 1996), pp. 43, 45. A compressed version of this article appeared as 'The West v the Rest', *Guardian*, 23 November 1996.
16 S.D. Krasner, 'Compromising Westphalia', *International Security* (20/3, Winter 1995/6).
17 S. Hoffman, 'The Politics and Ethics of Military Intervention', *Survival* (37/4, Winter 1995–6), p. 31.
18 SIPRI define a 'major armed conflict' as 'prolonged combat between the military forces of two or more governments, or of one government and at least one organized armed group, and incurring the battle-related deaths of at least 1000 people during the entire conflict': SIPRI, *Yearbook 1997: Armaments, Disarmament and International Security* (Oxford: Oxford University Press/SIPRI, 1997), pp. 17–30.
19 SIPRI, *Yearbook 1997*, p. 22.
20 Ibid.
21 SIPRI, *Yearbook 1996: Armaments, Disarmament and International Security* (Oxford: Oxford University Press/SIPRI, 1996), p. 21.
22 F. Halliday, 'The Gulf War 1990–91 and the Study of International Relations', *Review of International Studies* (20/2, April 1994), p. 112.

23 Waltz, 'The Emerging Structure of International Politics', p. 49.
24 'The Appeal of an Incoherent Ideology', *Financial Times*, 12 November 1994.
25 S. Sloan, *NATO's Future: Beyond Collective Defense,* McNair Paper no. 46 (Washington DC: INSS/NDU, December 1995), p. 21. I am grateful to Dr Stephen Elliot for his thoughts on egg custard.
26 As J.S. Duffield has pointed out, this assumption is as untested as it is popular: 'Explaining the Long Peace in Europe: The Contributions of Regional Security Regimes', *Review of International Studies* (20/4, October 1994), p. 370, n. 5.
27 For a concise discussion, see P. Collins, *Ideology after the Fall of Communism* (London: Boyars/Bowerdean, 1992).
28 An idea not without its critics; for a rounded discussion see J. MacMillan, 'Democracies Don't Fight: A Case of the Wrong Research Agenda?', *Review of International Studies* (22/3, July 1996).
29 F. Fukuyama, 'The End of History?', *The National Interest* (Summer 1989).
30 F. Fukuyama, *The End of History and the Last Man* (London: Hamish Hamilton, 1992), p. 328.
31 The phrase 'thoroughly improbable' is Hoffman's: 'The Politics and Ethics of Military Intervention', p. 32.
32 Fukuyama, *The End of History*, p. 330.
33 Ibid., p. 334.
34 Ibid., p. 332.
35 See Duffield, 'Explaining the Long Peace in Europe', pp. 378, 388.
36 J.E. Dougherty and R.L. Pfaltzgraff, *Contending Theories of International Relations* (Harper & Row, 1990), p. 480.
37 A.G. McGrew and M.J. Wilson, *Decision-Making: Approaches and Analysis* (Manchester University Press/Open University, 1982), p. 10.
38 The 'organizational process' and 'governmental (bureaucratic) politics' models come from Allison, who used them to challenge the authority of the 'Rational Actor' model: G.T. Allison, *Essence of Decision: Explaining the Cuban Missile Crisis* (New York: HarperCollins, 1971).
39 R.D. Asmus, R.D. Blackwill and F.S. Larrabee, 'Can NATO Survive?', *Washington Quarterly* (Spring 1996), p. 85.
40 The three phases are set out in McCalla, 'NATO's Persistence after the Cold War', p. 458.
41 For a comparison of international organizations and institutions, see C. Archer, *International Organizations,* 2nd edn (London: Routledge, 1992).
42 It is often asserted that one of NATO's most important functions has been to prevent two of its members – Greece and Turkey – fighting each other.
43 I am grateful to Dr Philip Towle for bringing the Dutch Barrier to my attention.

44 General John Shalikashvili, then Chairman of the US Joint Chiefs of Staff, quoted in 'Beyond the BUR', *Armed Forces Journal International*, March 1997.

45 G. Stix, 'Fighting Future Wars', *Scientific American*, December 1995, p. 76.

46 This is discussed in my *British Military Planning for the Defence of Germany, 1945–50* (London: Macmillan, 1996).

47 M. Carver, 'Britain, Alliances and Intervention', in M. Clarke and P. Sabin (eds), *British Defence Choices for the Twenty-First Century* (London: Brassey's, 1993), p. 28.

48 Sloan, *NATO's Future*, p. 2.

49 'Defending our Future', *Statement on the Defence Estimates 1993*, Cm2270 (London: HMSO, July 1993). See also M. Rifkind, 'Resources, Commitments and Capabilities: The Conundra of the Defence Debate', *Journal of the Royal United Services Institute* (138/4, August 1993), and P. Inge, 'The Capability-Based Army', *Journal of the Royal United Services Institute* (139/3, June 1994).

50 R. Fry, 'Operations in a Changed Strategic Environment', *Journal of the Royal United Services Institute* (140/3, June 1995), p. 34.

Chapter 3: Four paths to compromise

1 A. Menon, 'From Independence to Cooperation: France, NATO and European Security', *International Affairs* (71/1, January 1995), p. 22.

2 The agreement was to place the Eurocorps (including, therefore, its French contingent) under SACEUR's operational *command* in time of conflict. Previously, French troops taking part in NATO collective defence would have been merely under SACEUR's operational *control*. Militarily, the difference between command and control of a formation rests on the flexibility a commander has in using troops assigned to him; a battalion commander would have *command* of his infantry soldiers, but might only *control* artillery guns assigned to him, which might be redeployed elsewhere by the artillery commander. In the context of the relationship between France and NATO during the Cold War, France's preference for *control* ensured that the initiative behind, and ultimate command of, the deployment of French soldiers rested with the French government.

3 North Atlantic Council communiqué, Berlin, 3 June 1996 ('Berlin communiqué'); *NATO Review* (44/4, July 1996), pp. 30–5.

4 'NATO Acquires a European Identity', *The Economist*, 8 June 1996.

5 Quoted in 'Defence Deal Keeps All the Parties Happy', *Independent*, 4 June 1996.

6 S.N. Drew, 'From Berlin to Bosnia: NATO in Transition, 1989–1994', in C. Barry (ed.), *Reforging the Transatlantic Relationship* (Washington DC: NDU Press, 1996), p. 8.

7   See A.H. Cordesman, *US Defence Policy: Resources and Capabilities* (Whitehall Paper no. 24, London: RUSI, 1994), p. 7.

8   The 'Hague Platform' can be found in Western European Union, *The Reactivation of WEU: Statements and Communiqués, 1984 to 1987* (London: WEU, 1988), pp. 37–45.

9   Hague Platform, para. I/4.

10 W. van Eekelen, *The Security Agenda for 1996: Background and Proposals,* CEPS Paper no. 64 (Brussels, 1995), pp. 42–3.

11 S. Sloan, *NATO's Future: Beyond Collective Defense,* McNair Paper no. 46 (Washington DC: NDU/INSS, December 1995), p. 12.

12 S. Brown, *The Faces of Power: United States Foreign Policy from Truman to Clinton* (New York: Columbia University Press, 1994), p. 516.

13 Ibid., p. 589.

14 Ibid., p. 515.

15 P.R.S. Gebhard, *The United States and European Security,* Adelphi Paper no. 286 (London: IISS, February 1994), p. 4.

16 P. Zelikow, 'The Masque of Institutions', *Survival* (38/1, Spring 1996), p. 11.

17 C.L. Powell, 'The American Commitment to European Security', *Survival* (34/2, Summer 1992), p. 6. NB: '*inter*-regional crises' might be a typographical error; '*intra*-regional crises' would be consistent with the rest of this passage.

18 S. Cowper-Coles, 'From Defence to Security: British Policy in Transition', *Survival* (36/1, Spring 1994), p. 144.

19 J. Baylis, 'Britain and the Future of NATO', in M. Clarke and P. Sabin (eds), *British Defence Choices for the Twenty-First Century* (London: Brassey's, 1993), p. 13.

20 M. Carver, 'Britain, Alliances and Intervention', in Clarke and Sabin (eds), *British Defence Choices*, pp. 24–5.

21 'UK Aims at Compromise over European Forces', *Financial Times*, 15 May 1992.

22 'UK Seeks Role in European Defence Plans', *Financial Times*, 25 January 1994.

23 'UK Eyes Bigger Role in European Defense', *Defense News*, 27 January 1994.

24 'Britain Changes Tack to Back European Power Bloc in NATO', *The Times*, 28 October 1994.

25 Foreign and Commonwealth Office, *Memorandum on the United Kingdom Government's Approach to the Treatment of European Defence Issues at the 1996 Inter-Governmental Conference* (London: FCO, March 1996).

26 'Western Europe Looks to Southern Flank', *International Herald Tribune*, 16 May 1995.

27 'Europe's Big Battalions Begin to March Together', *Independent*, 22 February 1996.

28 'Major Warns on EU Defence Role', *Financial Times*, 24 February 1996.
29 Foreign and Commonwealth Office, *A Partnership of Nations: The British Approach to the European Union Intergovernmental Conference 1996* (London: HMSO, 1996), pp. 17–22.
30 R.P. Grant, 'France's New Relationship with NATO', *Survival* (38/1, Spring 1996), p. 59. For another excellent analysis of French security policy after the Cold War see Menon, 'From Independence to Cooperation'.
31 'US Agrees to Give Europe More Say in NATO Operations', *Financial Times*, 4 June 1996.
32 F. Charillon, 'France and NATO: Atlanticism as the Pursuit of Europe by other Means?', *Journal of the Royal United Services Institute* (141/6, December 1996), p. 46.
33 M. Legge, 'The Making of NATO's New Strategy', *NATO Review* (39/6, December 1991), p. 11.
34 Grant, 'France's New Relationship with NATO', p. 61.
35 Ibid., p. 58.
36 'Europe's Defence Dance', *Foreign Report*, 7 March 1996.
37 'French PM Suggests Independent EU Army', *Jane's Defence Weekly*, 20 March 1996, p. 11.
38 'France, Germany Push Greater EU Security Role', *Defense News*, 10 June 1996.
39 'Danke Schön: Shock Waves from French Defense Cuts Reverberate all the Way to Bonn', *Armed Forces Journal International*, June 1996.
40 Personal communication.
41 The subtleties and complexities of German views of Europe and its security are barely embraced in this section. See H. Mayer, 'Europe's Central Power: The German Debate over a Post-Cold War European Order', in R. Niblett and W. Wallace (eds), *Rethinking European Order* (provisional title, forthcoming).
42 T. Swann and S.R. Sloan, 'West European Attitudes toward the US Role in European Security', *CRS Report for Congress* (95–1200, 12 December 1995), p. 5.
43 For an illustration of the way in which German official statements have tried to reconcile these imperatives, see German Federal Ministry of Defence, *White Paper 1994*, particularly paras 410, 421 and 435.
44 H. De Santis, 'The Graying of NATO', in B. Roberts (ed.), *US Security in an Uncertain Era* (Cambridge, Mass.: MIT Press, 1993), p. 119.
45 See 'Franco-German Force Will be Operational by 1995, Bonn Says', *The Times*, 15 May 1995. The Franco-German Eurocorps enlarged upon an idea launched in January 1988, when Germany and France established a bilateral Joint Security and Defence Council and created a 4,000-man combined brigade. The brigade became operational in October 1990, although its operational effectiveness was always the subject of speculation.

46 'Europe's Big Battalions Begin to March Together', *Independent*, 22 February 1996.
47 'Europe's Defence Dance', *Foreign Report*, 7 March 1996.
48 'US and Europe Agree NATO Role', *The Times*, 4 June 1996.
49 P. Schmidt, 'ESDI: A German Analysis', in Barry (ed.), *Reforging the Transatlantic Relationship*, p. 39.
50 Ibid., p. 51.
51 Text of an address by V. Rühe to the Royal Institute of International Affairs and Konrad-Adenauer-Stiftung, Chatham House, London, 19 November 1996 (emphasis added).
52 'Danke Schön: Shock Waves from French Defense Cuts', *Armed Forces Journal International*, June 1996. See also 'France is Determined to Play a Central Role in Europe's Defence', *Jane's Defence Weekly*, 12 February 1997.
53 See J. Roper, evidence to House of Commons Select Committee on Defence, 'Western European Union', *Session 95–96, Fourth Report* (London: HMSO, 8 May 1996), p. 32.
54 Schmidt, 'ESDI', p. 52.

Chapter 4: Military adaptation: NATO's twenty-first-century triad

1 *London Declaration on a Transformed North Atlantic Alliance*, NATO, London, 5–6 July 1990.
2 *London Declaration*, para.14. Article 5 of the North Atlantic Treaty of 4 April 1949 contains an explicit commitment to joint defence of NATO territory *in Europe or North America*: 'The Parties agree that an armed attack against one or more of them in Europe or North America shall be considered an attack against them all and consequently they agree that, if such an armed attack occurs, each of them, in exercise of the right of individual or collective self-defence recognized by Article 51 of the Charter of the United Nations, will assist the Party or Parties so attacked by taking forthwith, individually and in concert with the other parties, such action as it deems necessary, including the use of armed force, to restore and maintain the security of the North Atlantic area.'
3 S.N. Drew, 'From Berlin to Bosnia: NATO in Transition, 1989–1994', in C. Barry (ed.), *Reforging the Transatlantic Relationship* (Washington DC: NDU Press, 1996), p. 4.
4 M. Legge, 'The Making of NATO's New Strategy', *NATO Review* (39/6, December 1991), p. 11.
5 *London Declaration,* para. 20.
6 The new force structure – known as MC 317 – would consist of *Reaction Forces* (*Immediate* and *Rapid*), *Main Defence Forces* and *Augmentation Forces*. See NATO communiqué M-DPC/NPG-1(91)38, 29 May 1991.
7 The four functions were: to provide a stable security environment in

Europe; to act as a forum for transatlantic discussion; to defend against aggression; to preserve the strategic balance in Europe. See NATO Communiqué M-1(91) 44, 7 June 1991.

8 *The Alliance's Strategic Concept* (MC 400/1) (Brussels: NATO, November 1991).

9 S. Sloan, *NATO's Future: Beyond Collective Defense,* McNair Paper no. 46 (Washington DC: INSS/NDU, December 1995), p. 10.

10 See *The Alliance's Strategic Concept,* paras 45–54.

11 J.R. Galvin, 'From Immediate Defence towards Long-term Stability', *NATO Review* (39/6, December 1991), p. 15.

12 R.H. Palin, *Multinational Military Forces: Problems and Prospects,* Adelphi Paper no. 294 (London: IISS, 1995), p. 15.

13 P.D. Miller, *Retaining Alliance Relevancy: NATO and the Combined Joint Task Force Concept,* National Security Papers no. 15 (Cambridge, Mass.: IFPA, 1994), p. 28.

14 Ibid., p. 29.

15 NATO communiqué DPC, 27 May 1992, para.10; *NATO Review* (40/3, June 1992), p. 35.

16 'Hanging Together in NATO: The Ongoing Review of Command Structures', *RUSI Newsbrief* (16/11, November 1996).

17 NATO communiqué M-DPC/NPG-1(95)57, 8 June 1995.

18 E. Foster, *NATO's Military in the Age of Crisis Management,* Whitehall Papers no. 29 (London: RUSI, 1995), p. 34.

19 V. Eide, 'The Military Dimension in the Transformed Alliance', *NATO Review* (40/4, August 1992), p. 23.

20 NATO Office of Information and Press, *NATO Handbook* (Brussels, October 1995), p. 164.

21 Cited in W.T. Johnsen, 'More Work in the Augean Stables? Reorganizing NATO's C2 Structures', *War Studies Journal* (1/1, Autumn 1996), p. 59 n. 12.

22 *NATO Handbook,* p. 166.

23 *Declaration of the Heads of State and Government,* Brussels, 10–11 January 1994; see *NATO Review* (42/1, February 1994), pp. 30–3.

24 I. Szönyi, 'Reform of the Alliance: Unfinished Business', in G. Bonvicini, M. Cremasco, R. Rummel and P. Schmidt (eds), *A Renewed Partnership for Europe* (Baden-Baden: Nomos/SWP, 1995), p. 212.

25 The NAC-DM meeting followed another meeting earlier in the day when NATO's defence ministers met in the established DPC/NPG forum – see NATO communiqué M-DPC/NPG-1(96)88, 13 June 1996.

26 NATO communiqué M-NAC(DM)-2(96)89, 13 June 1996.

27 'Simulating Crisis Response: US Atlantic Command Pioneers Joint Task Force Headquarters Staff Training', *Armed Forces Journal International,* October 1996.

28   Miller, *Retaining Alliance Relevancy*, p. 53.
29   C. Barry, 'ESDI: Toward a Bipolar Alliance?', in C. Barry (ed.), *Reforging the Transatlantic Relationship* (Washington DC: NDU Press, 1996), p. 76.
30   W. van Eekelen, *The Security Agenda for 1996: Background and Proposals,* CEPS Paper no. 64 (Brussels, 1995), p. 28.
31   NATO communiqué M-NAC(DM)-2(96)89, 13 June 1996 (emphases added).
32   Drew, 'From Berlin to Bosnia', p. 12.
33   M. Wörner, 'Shaping the Alliance for the Future', *NATO Review* (42/1, February 1994), p. 4.
34   R. Asmus, R. Kugler and S. Larrabee, 'What Will NATO Enlargement Cost?', *Survival* (38/3, Autumn 1996).
35   A. Karkoszka, quoted in 'Poland Urges NATO Not to Appease Russia', *Washington Post*, 17 March 1997.
36   NATO communiqué M-NAC-1(96)63, 3 June 1996.
37   'Defence Deal Keeps All the Parties Happy', *Independent*, 4 June 1996.
38   'Cold-shoulder Diplomacy', op-ed, *Washington Post*, 17 October 1996.
39   'Europe's New Order', *Financial Times*, 25 September 1996.
40   By now, a new suite of labels had emerged: MNC was replaced with 'Strategic Command'; MSC with 'Regional Command'; and PSC and sub-PSC with either 'Sub-Regional Command' (i.e. joint), or 'Component Command' (i.e. single-service). To avoid confusion, the old terms will be used for the remainder of this text.
41   'NATO Committee Devises New Headquarters Plan', *Defense News*, 25 November 1996.
42   M. Carver, 'Challenge to NATO Command System' (letter), *The Times*, 28 November 1996.
43   NATO communiqué M-NAC-2(96) 165, 10 December 1996.
44   NATO communiqué M-NAC(DM)-3(96)172, 18 December 1996.
45   See 'France is Determined to Play a Central Role in Europe's Defence', *Jane's Defence Weekly*, 12 February 1997; 'New Rift over NATO Threatened by France', *The Times*, 25 February 1997.
46   'NATO Chief Says Moscow Ready for Security Deal', *The Times*, 5 March 1997.
47   See 'Turkey Cries Foul over Treatment by Union', *European Voice*, 19 December 1996, and 'Turkey Insists on EU Entry as Price for Bigger NATO', *The Times*, 7 February 1997.
48   Unexpectedly, relations between Greece and Turkey took a step forward at Madrid, with the signature of a non-aggression pact: 'Greece and Turkey Surprise with Peace Pact', *Jane's Defence Weekly*, 16 July 1997.
49   'NATO: Who Will Join the Club?', *The Economist*, 7 June 1997.
50   'Chirac Bows to Anglo-US Deal', *The Times*, 9 July 1997.
51   'Franco-US Bickering Sours "Historic" Madrid Summit', *The Times*, 7 July 1997.

52 'A Bigger NATO: Europe Changes Shape', *The Economist*, 12 July 1997.
53 NATO communiqué M-DPC/NPG-1(96)88, 13 June 1996.
54 NATO communiqué M-NAC(DM)-2(96)89, 13 June 1996.
55 'NATO, CJTFs and IFOR', *Strategic Comments* (2/5, June 1996).
56 NATO communiqué M-DPC/NPG-2(96)173, 17 December 1996.
57 NATO communiqué M-NAC(DM)-3(96)172, 18 December 1996, paras 15–17.
58 It has been said that the 'NATO-Plus' Stabilization Force (SFOR) operation in Bosnia has seen over 20 different communications systems being used (personal communication).
59 *Madrid Declaration on Euro-Atlantic Security and Cooperation*, NATO press release M-1(97)81, 8 July 1997, para. 19.
60 D.C. Gompert and R.L. Kugler, *Rebuilding the Team: How to Get Allies to Do More in Defence of Common Interests* (Washington DC: RAND, September 1996), p. 3.
61 In EAPC, 'self-differentiation' ensures that 'partners will be able to decide for themselves the level and areas of cooperation with NATO': *Basic Document of the Euro-Atlantic Partnership Council*, NATO press release M-NACC-EAPC-1(97)66, 30 May 1997, para. 4.

Chapter 5: Testing the consensus

1 NATO communiqué M-NAC-1(96)63, 3 June 1996.
2 See, e.g., J.B. Steinberg, director of policy planning at the US State Department, speaking to the US Atlantic Council on 13 June 1996: United States Information Service (USIS), *Official Text*, 18 June 1996. The three objectives were also set out in a number of NATO communiqués in 1996: M-AC(DM)-2(96)89, 13 June 1996; M-NAC-2(96)165, 10 December 1996; M-NAC(DM)-3(96)172, 18 December 1996.
3 For the obstacles to ratification by the US Senate see 'Things Have Changed, George', *The Economist*, 12 July 1997.
4 'US and Europe Agree NATO Role', *The Times*, 4 June 1996.
5 USIS, *Washington File*, EUR504, 31 May 1996.
6 USIS, *Washington File*, EUR113, 3 June 1996.
7 USIS, *Washington File*, EUR203, 23 July 1996.
8 USIS, *Washington File*, EUR205, 4 June 1996.
9 See 'NATO Ministers Approve Plans for "New" NATO', *New York Times*, 4 June 1996; Steinberg, text of speech (USIS, *Official Text*), 18 June 1996; and 'NATO Gives Members Response Flexibility', *Washington Post*, 4 June 1996.
10 USIS, *Washington File*, EUR106, 17 June 1996.
11 'NATO Ministers Approve Plans for "New" NATO', *New York Times*, 4 June 1996.

12 USIS, *Washington File*, EUR203, 23 July 1996.
13 USIS, *Washington File*, EUR113, 3 June 1996.
14 USIS, *Washington File*, EUR204, 4 June 1996.
15 USIS, *Washington File*, EUR203, 23 July 1996.
16 'NATO Gives Members Response Flexibility', *Washington Post*, 4 June 1996.
17 NATODATA press briefing, 13 June 1996.
18 This was a particularly important point. If US leadership of a unified NATO remained unchallenged, then the problem of 'lending' US forces and equipment to a WEU-led operation could be circumvented. US forces might be deployed under the operational command of a European on a WEU-led CJTF, but since overall, strategic command of the operation would remain with SACEUR (always a US general), then US forces and equipment could be said to remain under ultimate US command. See USIS, *Washington File*, EUR205, 4 June 1996.
19 This stipulation effectively gave the US (and, for that matter, Turkey) a veto on any European aspirations.
20 It is interesting to note how little the EU features in official US comment on the security arrangements agreed at Berlin. Hunter, having stressed the importance of the WEU in the overall arrangement, could accept that the Berlin agreement would, indirectly, 'aid the European Union's development', but he did not discuss the possibility of direct cooperation between NATO and the EU. See USIS, *Washington File*, EUR203, 23 July 1996.
21 USIS, *Washington File*, EUR204, 4 June 1996.
22 P. Gordon, '"Europeanization" of NATO: A Convenient Myth', *International Herald Tribune*, 7 June 1996. For a similar interpretation see J. Eyal, quoted in 'A New Look for NATO', *Time*, 17 June 1996. The article proceeds to quote a US official's view that 'any boost to Europe's military self-image "will be a bonus".'
23 R.D. Asmus, R.D. Blackwill and F.S. Larrabee, 'Can NATO Survive?', *Washington Quarterly* (Spring 1996), p. 96.
24 J. Kornblum, speech to NATO public opinion seminar, January 1995; USIS, *Official Text*, 31 January 1995.
25 See USIS, *Washington File*, EUR101, 3 June 1996; EUR205, 4 June 1996; EUR 106, 17 June 1996.
26 Anthony Lake, Oscar Iden lecture (unpublished text), Georgetown University, Washington DC, 8 October 1996.
27 D.C. Gompert, 'Sharing the Burdens of Global Security', Occasional Paper no. 1 (Washington DC: Henry L. Stimson Center and Overseas Development Council, August 1996).
28 Ibid., p. 25.
29 Asmus et al., 'Can NATO Survive?', p. 92.
30 Ibid., pp. 79, 88.

31 D.C. Gompert and R.L. Kugler, 'Rebuilding the Team: How to Get Allies to Do More in Defense of Common Interests', RAND Issue Paper (Washington DC, September 1996), pp. 1–3.

32 'Defence Deal Keeps All the Parties Happy', *Independent*, 4 June 1996.

33 M. Rifkind, text of address to WEU Assembly, Paris, 5 June 1996 (URL: http://www.fco.gov.uk).

34 See 'Defence Deal Keeps All the Parties Happy', *Independent*, 4 June 1996; 'NATO Acquires a European Identity', *The Economist*, 8 June 1996; 'US Agrees to Give Europe More Say in NATO Operations', *Financial Times*, 4 June 1996, and 'US and Europe Agree NATO Role', *The Times*, 4 June 1996.

35 J. Goulden, 'NATO Approaching Two Summits: the UK Perspective' (text of an address to the Royal United Services Institute, 3 October 1996), *Journal of the Royal United Services Institute* (141/6, December 1996). For comparable views from the UK Ministry of Defence see R. Hatfield, 'The UK's Approach to the European Security and Defence Identity', *Journal of the Royal United Services Institute* (142/2, April 1997).

36 'NATO Gives Members Response Flexibility', *Washington Post*, 4 June 1996.

37 V. Rühe, unpublished text of address to the Royal Institute of International Affairs and the Konrad-Adenauer-Stiftung, Chatham House, 19 November 1996.

38 H. Freiherr von Richthofen, 'The Evolution of NATO from a German Point of View' (text of an address to the Royal United Services Institute, 22 November 1996), *Journal of the Royal United Services Institute* (141/6, December 1996).

39 The differences between the British and German approaches to European defence and security are explained entertainingly in E. Foster and P. Schmidt, *Anglo-German Relations in Security and Defence: Taking Stock,* Whitehall Papers no. 39 (London: RUSI, 1997) p. 17.

40 Quoted in 'NATO Gives Members Response Flexibility', *Washington Post*, 4 June 1996.

41 Quoted in Royal United Services Institute, *International Security Review 1997* (London: RUSI, 1997), p. 8.

42 Texts of speeches by H. de Charette and J. Chirac, 3 December 1996, in French Foreign Ministry, *French Presidency of WEU: Statements* (URL: www.france.diplomatie.fr/actual/ueo).

43 Record of a press conference given by President Chirac in Prague, 3 April 1997 (URL: www.france.diplomatie.fr/cgi-bin). The same warning had earlier been given by French defence minister Charles Millon at the meeting of NATO defence ministers in Bergen, Norway, on 25 September 1996.

44 'A Bigger NATO: Europe Changes Shape', *The Economist*, 12 July 1997.

45 J. Casanova, quoted in Charillon, 'France and NATO', p. 47.
46 De Charette, text of 3 December 1996; Chirac, text of 3 December 1996.
47 'Quick march! Who says?', *The Economist*, 22 March 1997.
48 M. Smith, 'The Commission and External Relations', in G. Edwards and
    D. Spence (eds), *The European Commission* (Harlow: Longman, 1994),
    p. 249.
49 See S. Nuttall, 'The Commission and Foreign Policy-making', in Edwards
    and Spence (eds), *The European Commission*.
50 Ibid., p. 295.
51 M. Holland, *European Common Foreign Policy: From EPC to CFSP Joint
    Action and South Africa* (London: Macmillan, 1995), p. 12.
52 H. Grabbe and K. Hughes, *Eastward Enlargement of the European Union,*
    Special Paper (London: RIIA, February 1997).
53 For an assessment of various proposals to improve CFSP see C. Grant,
    Strength in Numbers: Europe's Foreign and Defence Policy (London:
    Centre for European Reform, 1996).
54 High-level Group of Experts on the CFSP, *European Security Policy
    Towards 2000: Ways and Means to Establish Genuine Credibility* (Brus-
    sels, 19 December 1994).
55 European Parliament Committee on Foreign Affairs, Security and Defence
    Policy, *Report on Progress in Implementing the CFSP, January–December
    1995* (PE 216.369/fin., 30 May 1996).
56 DG1A briefing note IA/A/CMR D(96), 21 June 1996.
57 F. Cameron, 'European Security – a Commission Perspective', *Journal of
    the Royal United Services Institute* (142/2, April 1997), p. 54.
58 'EU Could Take Lead in Bosnia Next Year', *Financial Times*, 4 May 1996.
59 WEU Birmingham Declaration, 7 May 1996, para. 7 (URL: http://
    fco.gov.uk/weu/declaration.htm); emphasis added.
60 'US and Europe Agree NATO Role', *The Times*, 4 June 1996.
61 'European Union: On Track', *The Economist*, 31 May 1997.
62 *Draft Treaty of Amsterdam*, CONF/4001/97, Brussels, 19 June 1997.
    Before its publication, *The Economist* had expected the Treaty to be
    'comprehensively incomprehensible': 'Driven to Distraction by the
    Esoteric Art of Treaty Revision', 31 May 1997.
63 'London to Challenge "Dog's Dinner" Treaty', *The Times*, 26 June 1997.
64 *Draft Treaty of Amsterdam*, Article J.7, para.1 (emphasis added). The TEU
    had used 'eventual' rather than 'progressive'; the latter term suggests
    dynamism, but is more open-ended.
65 *Draft Treaty of Amsterdam*, Article J.7, para.2. This form of words is
    borrowed from the WEU Petersberg Declaration, 19 June 1992.
66 See G. Messervy-Whiting, 'Europe's Security and Defence Identity: The
    Western European Union's Operational Development', *Journal of the
    Royal United Services Institute* (142/2, April 1997).

67 The 1984 Rome Declaration and 1987 Hague Platform can be found in Western European Union, *The Reactivation of WEU: Statements and Communiqués, 1984 to 1987* (London: Secretariat-General of WEU, 1988).

68 J. Paganon, 'Western European Union's Pivotal Position between the Atlantic Alliance and the European Union', in A. Deighton (ed.), *Western European Union 1954–1997: Defence, Security, Integration* (Oxford: St Antony's College, 1997), pp. 94–6.

69 N. Gnesotto, 'Common European Defence and Transatlantic Relations', *Survival* (38/1, Spring 1996), p. 28.

70 P. Schmidt, 'ESDI: A German Analysis', in C. Barry (ed.), *Reforging the Transatlantic Relationship* (Washington DC: NDU Press, 1996), p. 44.

71 'Arms Competition Rips at NATO's Military Fabric', *Defense News*, 14 April 1997.

72 'Statement by Eurogroup Ministers', *NATO Review*, February 1994, p. 23.

73 See W. Walker and P. Gummett, 'Britain and the European Armaments Market', *International Affairs* (65/3, Summer 1989).

74 'A Survey of Military Aerospace', *The Economist*, 3 September 1994, p. 18.

75 IISS, *Military Balance 1996/97* (London: IISS/Oxford University Press, 1996), p. 306.

76 See M. Leibstone, 'Corporate Merger-Mania: Good or Bad for US Defence?', *Military Technology*, June 1996.

77 'Lockheed Gobbles Another', *The Economist*, 5 July 1997.

78 'The Boeing–McDonnell Douglas Merger: Omen or Opportunity?', *RUSI Newsbrief* (17/1, January 1997).

79 'Enter McBoeing', *The Economist*, 21 December 1996. See also 'A Survey of the Global Defence Industry', *The Economist*, 14 June 1997.

80 'EU Struggles to Get Defence Act Together', *Financial Times*, 11 December 1996.

81 'A Survey of the Global Defence Industry', *The Economist*, 14 June 1997.

82 'Raytheon's Rise', *The Economist*, 18 January 1997.

83 L. Martin, quoted in 'Skepticisim Greets New WEU Arms Agency', *Defense News*, 25 November 1996.

84 'GEC and BAe Are Tipped for £16bn Merger', *Sunday Times*, 23 February 1997.

85 'Western Firms Surge into Central, Eastern Europe', *Defense News*, 23 June 1997.

86 'Industry must Wait for Eastern European Fighter Buys', *Defense News*, 4 August 1997. Romania and Slovenia have both begun discussions with the United States over aircraft purchases: 'Romania, Slovenia Seek US Fighter Briefings', *Jane's Defence Weekly*, 6 August 1997. Lockheed Martin also anticipates a healthy market for C^4I and ground-based radar systems: 'NATO Enlargement to Boost C^4I System Sales', *Jane's Defence Contracts*, July 1997.

87 See 'US Questions Europe's Commitment on Self-defense', *Defense News*, 30 June 1997.

Chapter 6: Conclusion

1 The Volvo V70 can thrust its occupants in air-bagged, impact-protected safety and air-conditioned, unruffled comfort to around 150 miles per hour in just a few seconds, albeit not in Britain.
2 USIS, *Washington File*, EUR106, 17 June 1996 (emphasis added).

Chatham House Papers

THE ROYAL INSTITUTE OF INTERNATIONAL AFFAIRS

forthcoming

Heather Grabbe and Kirsty Hughes

Enlarging the EU Eastwards

Successful eastward enlargement of the EU will be critical to ensuring stability and prosperity for post-Cold War Europe. But it raises difficult issues for the EU and the applicant countries of central and eastern Europe (CEE). Can the EU reform to cope with 25 or more members? Which CEE countries will join, and when? How can we ensure that enlargement brings the economic and security benefits expected of it?

This comprehensive study examines in detail the political, economic and security implications of eastward enlargement for both East and West. The authors present new analyses of the policy issues, including the EU budget and institutional reform, and of the economic integration likely before and after accession. There is also a detailed assessment of the pre-accession strategy proposed in 'Agenda 2000'.

Based on an extensive series of interviews with key political actors across Europe, this study provides an informed overview of attitudes both within the EU and in the applicant countries.

128 pp   ISBN 1 85567 525 0 (*hb*)   £27.50 / US$44.95
          ISBN 1 85567 526 9 (*pb*)   £11.99 / US$15.95

February 1998   RIIA/Pinter